WAIT
A DIARY OF L
IN PREG
Ellen Judith

SOME ADVANCE REVIEWS

"In these pages a brave, perceptive woman finds the words to bring alive the powerful and often conflicting emotions and tensions in relationships associated with miscarriage and pregnancy. She explores her own identity as she becomes a mother and records what was for her a spiritual journey. This book is unique. Don't miss it!"

Sheila Kitzinger
Author, *The Complete Book of Pregnancy and Childbirth;* and *Homebirth and Other Alternatives to Hospital*

"Ms. Reich does an excellent job in sharing the sly and sometimes insidious workings of one mind, body, and soul during the transition to motherhood. Her writing is sometimes lyrical, always honest, and consistently well-written. The unexpected strength in this book is its poignant rendering about prospective motherhood."

Lynne Bravo Rosewater, PhD
Clinical Psychologist in Private Practice
Beachwood, Ohio

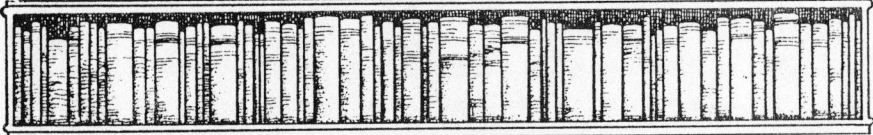

Waiting
A Diary of Loss and Hope in Pregnancy

HAWORTH Women's Studies
Ellen Cole, PhD and Esther Rothblum, PhD
Senior Co-Editors

New, Recent, and Forthcoming Titles:

When Husbands Come Out of the Closet by Jean Schaar Gochros

Prisoners of Ritual: An Odyssey into Female Circumcision in Africa by Hanny Lightfoot-Klein

Foundations for a Feminist Restructuring of the Academic Disciplines edited by Michele Paludi and Gertrude A. Steuernagel

Hippocrates' Handmaidens: Women Married to Physicians by Esther Nitzberg

Waiting: A Diary of Loss and Hope in Pregnancy by Ellen Judith Reich

God's Country: A Case Against Theocracy by Sandy Rapp

Women and Aging: Celebrating Ourselves by Ruth Raymond Thone

A Woman's Odyssey into Africa: Tracks Across a Life by Hanny Lightfoot-Klein

Women's Conflicts About Eating and Sexuality: The Relationship Between Food and Sex by Rosalyn M. Meadow and Lillie Weiss

Anorexia Nervosa and Recovery: A Hunger for Meaning by Karen Way

Waiting
A Diary of Loss and Hope in Pregnancy

Ellen Judith Reich

Harrington Park Press
An Imprint of The Haworth Press, Inc.
New York • London • Norwood (Australia)

ISBN 0-918393-88-4

Published by

Harrington Park Press, an imprint of The Haworth Press, Inc., 10 Alice Street, Binghamton, NY 13904-1580

Cover design by Marshall Andrews.

Library of Congress Cataloging-in-Publication Data

Reich, Ellen Judith.
    Waiting : a diary of loss and hope in pregnancy / by Ellen Judith Reich.
      p. cm.
    Includes index.
    ISBN 0-918393-88-4 (pbk.)
    1. Miscarriage — Psychological aspects. 2. Reich, Ellen Judith — Health. 3. Pregnant women — United States — Biography. 4. Anxiety. 5. Pregnant women — Psychology. I. Title.
RG648.R39   1991
618.3'92'092 — dc20
[B]
                                                             91-2249
                                                                  CIP

*Dedicated
to my family
old and new*

ABOUT THE AUTHOR

Ellen Judith Reich, JD, is a writer, lawyer, and new mother. A journalist and journal keeper, she turned the spotlight inward to cope with the losses of two miscarriages and examine her fear of change and loss of control. She graduated Phi Beta Kappa from Vassar College and earned her law degree from George Washington University. A former reporter for *The Charleston Gazette* and director of a battered women's program, she is now staying at home writing and caring for her son.

Acknowledgements

There are many people I would like to thank for seeing me through this project. First and foremost, thanks to Rick and Joey for their unyielding love and support. Elaine New and Nancy Donehower helped immensely through their friendship and the guidance and editing they provided. Thanks to Ruth Messenger, Leslie Wyatt, Karen Gantt, Jane Serling, and Mara Gabriel for reading and feedback, and thanks to the staff at The Haworth Press, especially Esther Rothblum, Ellen Cole, Jim Ice, Ida Walker, and Eric Roland. I would also like to extend thanks to John Friedman and to The Circle Weavers. And finally, thanks to so many others who have influenced my life in ways large and small.

Note: On occasion, names have been changed to protect privacy.

February 11

We saw the heartbeat. It was barely there. But the sonographer pointed it out, and Rick saw it and is on cloud nine. All I saw was this tiny white line blinking. I feel reassured, but not completely. I guess I'm just a worrywart. Maybe at 12 weeks (actually 12 1/2, on March 10) I'll feel better. Dr. Fried said they still may not be able to hear the heartbeat then, but it sounds like they might check it out with ultrasound again if they don't. Fried also said that once they find a heartbeat, chances of miscarriage go from about 20% to 3%. That's certainly good news. Now I have to try to study law for the bar.

February 17

The nausea has returned. It never fully left, but the attacks had begun to wane. Rather than hit full force with breakfast and last until bedtime, it would arrive a bit later each day. Yesterday my stomach felt fine until 5 o'clock. Then wham. A new instant aversion was created. The frozen yogurt that had been so satisfying before is repulsive now. (At least the chocolate flavor — which is probably well and good. Too bad the system doesn't reject only less-than-good-for-you foods. Peach and vanilla yogurt still seem fine.) But my system has been forced off the last six months of lacto-ovo vegetarianism. None of it appealed, most of it began to repulse, yet I can still keep down tuna fish and turkey.

The day is gorgeous. First hint of spring in the mild air. The birds are rediscovering the feeder. Put out a month ago but left empty for a week, the flocks that had descended fled to food sites unknown. Refilled, it's taken a few days for the birds to return. The chickadees and the starlings were the first back. Only one fat squirrel has shown himself and, miraculously, he doesn't try to scale the tree to the feeders, but keeps his bushy tail on the ground. Maybe it's the surrounding woods — he has easier smorgasbords elsewhere.

The nausea is systemic: not one, neat, swift and purging vomiting in the toilet. My heavy queasiness teases me for hours, plays at my nerves, driving me into the bathroom with dry heaves that shake my entire body, bringing tears to my eyes and agonizing breathlessness. And who wants to talk about it? The gory details of an out-of-kilter digestive system. Who even wants to hear about it? No one. It's like bathroom habits — you need to be elderly and ill before you forget or ignore social protocol and begin giving detailed accounts of the exit paths and problems of your food. And I am neither elderly nor ill. Not ill? How can that be?

I'm pregnant.

"Ah," people glow. Cheerful, serene, buoyant, hopeful. Planning the future and reveling in the miracle. Women encourage you, promising the problems will pass and that you will forget this stage. Women in the same stage groan with you. Such wisdom must be true or many, many families would be curtailed after the first birth. How many others groan through the miasma, begging God for twins or triplets, so they never have to do this again?

The entire experience is so startling to me, a woman who likes to be in control, a woman whose body has given her little grief before pregnancy came around. Periods were painless. The one time menstrual cramps struck, I was sure I had appendicitis. *This* is what other women go through each month, I thought, with astonishment, from my bed. I was only 16 then. Three years into womanhood and thirteen years before I felt severe cramps again — the cramps of a year ago as I miscarried our first baby.

February 19

One p.m. and so far the nausea is at bay. I didn't get out of bed until 11:30, furthering my daily impersonation of a tree sloth and moving in the slowest of slow mo'. Anything to feel better. My nighttime sleeping has shifted from my typical deep, sound, almost comatose slumber to a very light doze in which I am sensitive to Rick's every little move. It's only during the morning hours after he leaves that I slip into a mixture of sound sleep and wild REM dreaming.

Normally, most of my dreams fade quickly or are already forgotten when I wake. But the last month! Well, just truly bizarre. Dreams of lust. Dreams of blood and murder and decapitated chickens. Dreams of boats. Dreams of the house falling apart — literally. Dreams of my family (birth family) bringing new furniture that I don't like into this house. The dreams come every night, long and complicated. I could easily record them in the mornings, but I'm not sure I want to remember them all!

When the nausea clings to me, I keep imagining the cancer scenes in all the movies I've ever witnessed. Not because I think there's anything wrong with me. Only because I keep thinking, "I feel like I'm in chemotherapy." Perhaps this is a cruel insult from a healthy pregnant woman (everything aglow ahead of her) to one fighting death with drugs, but I feel totally shot through with alien forces disrupting my body. I have no appetite, yet I know I need to eat. I feel nauseous on an empty stomach; I feel nauseous on a full stomach, with no break in between. I retch up what I put down, and when I put nothing down it's even worse. I retch and heave, wave upon wave, on an empty stomach, saliva pouring from my mouth and water from my eyes, desperate for a deep breath or two to help me stop.

The birds are finally back — in droves. But if I stand too close to the window they flee in one movement, hiding for longer than I can wait. So I haven't yet figured out how long they stay in the trees, biding their time to ensure their safety. The cardinals — one male and one female — are the most cautious. They returned today. They were regulars before I let the feeder go empty. Yet they've never sat in the little tree which hosts the food, nor stepped on the feeder itself. They collect their food from the seeds fallen to the ground. I think we've attracted a goldfinch too, but it still wears its winter feathers, very muddy, with a vague pattern and emerging yellow. The chickadees dominate, with their white and black markings. Some soft-colored tufted titmice, with crowns shaped like cardinals, also visit. I recognize woodpeckers in the trees, but as my Peterson's bird book is still packed up in the garage from the October move, most of the feathered wonders remain unidentified. The boxes are too heavy for me. I can lift them, but I'm not supposed to, and Rick said he'd take all of my book boxes up to my office tonight. That will be quite a project; there are at least fifteen. It will take me a lot longer than an evening to unpack them.

The disabling effect of the nausea has another side, a side that keeps me in an emotional spin. As long as I feel it, I must still be pregnant, right? I'm not even sure past experience shows that to be correct. But every awful day seems to give Rick a small boost of confidence. He's too good a person to worry aloud if I have a good day. He's just pleased that maybe I'm finally through that phase (even though I have a month to go in the first trimester). We know there are no rules. There are no guarantees. Some women are lucky enough never to have the nausea, to go through the whole first three months with barely the knowledge of pregnancy. Some are nauseous for nine months.

Today the birds returned 45 minutes after fearful flight.

February 22

The day before the bar exam I'm no longer taking. I'm already a lawyer, technically speaking. I've been one for almost six years. I just never wanted to practice. I realized that by the third year of law school. I worked as a journalist instead. A bit of a patchwork career. I left daily newspaper life after three years for self-employment: a contract to write a small book about juvenile law in West

Virginia (my post-law-school home for three years) and a house-and pet-sitting business opened with a friend. We organized, advertised, and oversaw; others sat.

Then Rick and I reached the decision to leave the state. We wanted to remain in a tranquil place but wanted one with more opportunities for us and our future family. Figuring that the longer we stayed, the harder it would be to go, we pulled out all the stops. We researched, found jobs, sold our house, and moved — all within four months. Fate must be with us, we marvelled, to pull off something so complicated and potentially traumatic in such a rapid and flawless fashion. Rick had entered the world of private law practice, and I renewed a longtime interest in battered women and became a program director at a private social services agency.

Less than a month after moving to North Carolina, we stopped using contraception. I'd gone off the pill in July, and we had been waiting a few months to make sure my body was adjusting to normalcy. We took no chances, we did everything right. Never a smoker and rarely a drinker, I forswore any substance of possible danger. Once actively trying to conceive, I weathered any cold symptoms I got, no over-the-counter drugs either. I ate healthfully. I walked. I was healthy and 29.

So we began trying to conceive. After two months, we did. We were ecstatic. That was certainly easy. Always a little in doubt after so many years of trying *not* to get pregnant, I wondered if the machinery would really work, those female parts that asserted themselves in good working order more than 16 years ago with my first menstrual flow.

We were in California visiting Rick's family for the holidays when we affirmed the first pregnancy. I was late, and one home pregnancy test the prior week came out negative. The 23rd of December, we sneaked around a Los Angeles drugstore, surreptitiously buying another test. For those few days of the visit, we were staying with his father and we weren't ready to tell anyone what might have been going on. I barely slept that night, I was so excited and nervous. Despite the prior test, I just knew I was pregnant.

I cut way down on my fluids that evening, trying to get my morning urine at a concentration where the HCL couldn't be missed. I awoke early, very unusual for me, and headed for the bathroom.

Rick was awake, too. Fifteen minutes. I sat on the toilet seat, trying to read, with my watch in my hands, mostly staring at the two little spheres suspended in the chemical mix. Was that bottom one turning blue? God, but it was! After five minutes the edges had a tinge. From the outside in, it turned its magic color as the top sphere stayed white. I waited the full 15 minutes. Then I shyly burst out, giddy with a shit-eating grin on my face, "Does this look blue to you?" "It sure does," he said. We were ecstatic.

His father, Richard, and Richard's wife, Barbara, had left for work before the start of the test. I had waited that long. Richard was to return around noon. It was 8:00 a.m., the day before Christmas. I was dying to call my mother and brothers in New Jersey, but out of kilter with the news myself, I thought it was three hours earlier rather than later and didn't want to wake up anybody at 5:00 a.m. By 10:30 I realized the error, decided my mind was turning completely to mush, and reached my family. They were predictably pleased. My brothers seemed especially tickled. There are no grandchildren on my side of the family yet.

Despite my excitement, I felt then, as now, somewhat alone. For pregnancy questions or reassurance or camaraderie, there has been no one to turn to, period. Of three sisters-in-law on Rick's side, only one has chosen to have children and she and her husband adopted. My mother, now in her 70s, was 39 when she had my oldest brother and 42 by the time I came along as the caboose. She claims not to remember too much of her pregnancies. There must be selective memory at work though, because first she tells me she never experienced any nausea while pregnant. Later she tells me how, when she was ghastly sick on a European trip while pregnant with her first, my father kept telling her it was all in her head (an idea she didn't readily accept).

But pregnancy supporters? At that time, none of my close friends had children. So I read. A lot. K. C. Cole's *What Only A Mother Can Tell You About Having A Baby* was like finding a roomful of pregnant friends. It helped.

But the joy carried me along. We had conceived! We returned home by the new year. The only big change I noticed so far was fatigue and tender breasts. My mother came down for the big eve (always more of a family night for me than a public party night), and the nausea rolled in for the first time.

It was hard to be at work. Since I'd only been there four months I didn't want anyone to know until as late as possible. I felt guilty getting pregnant so quickly after starting a new job especially when, in my heart, I knew I'd want to be home with the baby. It wasn't fair to my co-workers. And I certainly didn't want to be treated as a lame duck, so I knew that part of my life would not be shared until much closer to the birth. And maybe I would even take the advice I'd heard so often: simply take the maternity leave and decide then. I might change my mind and want to return to work.

But being in a new area where my support and friends were as yet almost exclusively at work, made keeping quiet very hard. My fatigue was not lost on all, and many wondered if I might be pregnant. When the subject came up, I'd always say with a smile, "We're working on it." So by the time everything happened, not everyone was totally surprised. At least not by the fact of my pregnancy.

And I started out today writing about taking the bar! To make that short, I thought I'd get certified locally to keep my options open. As I was taking a sabbatical from work for an indefinite time (i.e., unemployed), the timing for the exam seemed perfect. Three weeks into the two-month course of study, I find I'm pregnant. For the third time. I will forge on, I say. I'll take care of myself but I'll do the best I can on the exam.

My body defeated me.

I hate not being in control, and here I was thrown to the winds on two major counts. First, I could not follow the necessary discipline for study because of fatigue and nausea. I held on until a week before the exam. But by then taking practice exams confirmed my fears. I was not up to passing level. A bitter shock. Academically, intellectually, I've never failed anything. I wrestled with the thought. I did not want to abstain from the exam simply because of *fear* of failure. If I failed, I failed. That shouldn't stop me from trying. I realized it wasn't fear. I was afraid I'd fail when I took the Maryland bar the summer after law school, and I felt that would be agony. Much of my entire purpose for taking it then was to prove to the world I could practice law if I wanted to, but I simply didn't want to. I had a fear that people might think I wasn't a practicing lawyer because I wasn't capable. Already many were incredulous. "Why give up all that money?" It was that blatant. If I failed then, my motivation for taking it again would be low. I didn't care *that* much, and I could not risk failing twice. Besides, I found I loved being a reporter. It suited my needs at the time.

This time around, I realized I wasn't simply suffering from a fear of failure. Instead, I had to face the sad, frustrating truth that I wasn't well enough prepared and that better preparation had been beyond my control.

The second fear was a reality, a question, spinning headlong out of my control. Would I even be having a baby?

February 24

One day last week I had cramps. Not very painful, no spotting, but recognizable as cramps. I hadn't slept well the night before, so I stayed in bed all morning, drowsing, dreaming, the cramps intermittent. I talked to Rick. He wanted me to call the doctor. They seemed better, so I hedged, bought time, and went for my regular (though slower these days) swim. I still felt OK but decided perhaps another blood test would do.

My doctor has monitored my progesterone level with blood tests in these early weeks. My history isn't consistent with spontaneous abortion due to progesterone deficiency, but that's his specialty and we want all the angles covered. I am, however, paranoid about taking progesterone. And what good are the doctor's reassurances? Zip. What doctor knew thalidomide would deform children? Or that DES would be associated with cervical cancer and infertility when these baby girls grew up? I am not persuaded by the fact that this is purely natural progesterone, not a synthetic match. I'm sure I would be more worried if it was synthetic, but my concern is with creating a hormone imbalance. If the acceptable first trimester progesterone levels range between 9 and 47, perhaps my level of 20 is proper for my body and my fetus.

As the doctor explained it, the progesterone primarily keeps the uterus from expelling the fetus. It doesn't assist in fetal development. My prior babies aborted, according to the ultrasounds, three weeks and four weeks, respectively, after development ceased. This is inconsistent with the problem of progesterone deficiency. A test after the second miscarriage, an endometrial biopsy, also looked at the levels of progesterone built up in my normal cycle and came back A-OK.

It was funny. At the time of the second miscarriage, when the doctors did this test and another called the lupus anticoagulant test (checking to see if I harbored some latent form of lupus), I was disappointed that both came back normal! Both problems, if found, had a proposed cure: take natural progesterone shots or vaginal suppositories for the first trimester if test one was a problem, and take one baby aspirin per day if test two indicated a problem.

Given how I feel, and have always felt, about taking anything during pregnancy, such a welcoming reaction seems odd. But I so desperately wanted to know why I had miscarried. I needed a reason. A cause. A peg. Something this always-in-control person could fix.

But no, I'm testing out normal all the way.

So now, nine weeks into my third pregnancy, I had cramps. I didn't want progesterone, but I didn't want to lose the baby either (even if my history didn't support this as the reason in the past). My progesterone levels have been testing out as acceptable, but not stellar. So I thought let's go give it another check. Ask them to draw another sample. If it's fallen, get the supplement.

The receptionist, nurses, aides — everybody was nice. They don't think I'm being paranoid by showing up on their doorstep, which makes me a little more nervous. Instead of just drawing the blood, they say the doctor will take a look at me. I'm really worried now. I just walk in, unannounced, with no appointment, no spotting, but a history of miscarriages, and the doctor will examine me?!? I know this is good, certainly a sign of good doctors, and I wait nearly an hour until I can be seen. I think that it's a good thing I've decided not to take the bar exam after all, or I would be in a total panic. Afraid of miscarrying and robbed of precious and necessary study hours.

The doctor pronounces that everything is looking good inside and agrees that another blood test is the way to go. Since the results take two days, he suggests I just relax for the rest of that day. But if the cramps get worse or are not gone by the next day, I'm to come back and they'll go ahead with the progesterone shot prior to getting the results.

I will the cramps to stay away. They do. Who knows why?

I find progesterone an interesting thing. Even though it is "perfectly safe" (been used 10 to 15 years, although not enough time for those little babies to fully grow up yet, I note), it does have one admitted side effect. It tends to suppress the body's natural production of the hormone. So it appears to me, once they start you on weekly shots, at least until the placenta takes over manufacture in the fourth month, you are on the shots. Your body stops kicking in.

Well, fine. I can worry my ears off if I want to. What of the apparent choice of lose the baby or take the shot? No contest. I take the shot. I think.

The question has been postponed by another doctor in the joint practice. When my results came in, I was scared. Two weeks before, I measured at 20.7. Now I hit only 18.9. My very first measure at five weeks was only 17.7. Surely I would need the drug. But my regular doctor wasn't in that day. I talked with a nurse. She said she'd talk with one of the other doctors. Twenty minutes later she called back. As long as I wasn't cramping any more (I wasn't) and I wasn't spotting (I wasn't), 18.9 was close enough to 20.7 that this doctor was most inclined to let well enough alone, as long as I felt OK with that (I did). Medical authority to back up my intuitive bent. If anything in my condition changed, however, don't hesitate to call immediately. Thanks. I will do that.

Yet another area OB my husband conferred with when we were in an earlier panic about my progesterone levels (week #2 reading was 17.5 compared to the original 17.7) said something memorable, if not exactly reassuring. "Dealing with the first trimester of pregnancy is a lot like black magic. We don't really know what's best or what makes it all tick." Those first 12 weeks are tentative and you're much on your own was the message.

The cramps went away. Every panty has been unmarked, every

toilet tissue clean. It is impossible not to look. Every time. Sometimes I wipe twice, just to be sure.

Faith is hard to find. Innocence, long gone.

Today is the second and final day of the bar exam I'm not taking.
Why is a small part of me still second-guessing that decision? What
was the real motivation for taking it this time? I can't prioritize. To
fill my time with something productive? Yes. A built-in timetable
and resultant discipline. To keep my options open? Sure. Hard to
argue with that one. Ego? To be able to say "I'm a lawyer" if I
wish, without feeling a need to add some explanation of accuracy
("In Maryland, not here") even if I still wasn't practicing. Yes,
that's part of it. And as insurance. Yes, a large part.

Insurance? Yes. Suppose Rick gets hit by a car (a more common
worry than "suppose we get divorced"). I'm fortunate enough to
have significant money of my own, even enough to live simply,
without a job, on my own. But not enough to keep living here
without work, not enough to take care of me and children. Suppose
some day a different form of reality greets my days — grimmer, sad-
der, grittier, more demanding. I want to be ready to get that lawyer
job I've never really wanted. But, I tell myself, if grim reality demands some nine to five (or eight to seven) butt kicking, I'll handle
it then. It would be harder, sure, but I could work and study up at
the same time. Many do. Or I could find some other sort of job. I
guess "lawyer" just looks like it would pay the most in the simplest
way.

So I've let my insurance policy lapse.

The nausea seems somewhat better. At least today. So far. God,
how cautious I've become!

Yesterday I became infuriated while browsing in a local bookstore, a favorite pastime of mine. Several reasons brought me in
yesterday. Two gifts to buy and another investigation of the pregnancy books. I must have 20 such books by now, owned or bor-
rowed. I see little new information in these books. I am a well-
educated pregnant patient. But I look for new information on the
nausea anyway. Reaffirming predictions of its length. Tips on making it better. Crackers. Yes, I try that. But eating them in bed before

getting up seems worse for me. Club soda was a new suggestion, and using it to dilute fruit juice was new. Good. I already know apples and apple juice are helpful. But cheese, a long-time favorite, seems to make the nausea worse, as has milk, another favorite. My six months of vegetarian diet has gone down the tubes recently. Vegetarianism is extremely boring if you're not cooking and, besides, I wasn't keeping most of it down. So I'm eating meats and tuna fish again, with better success, while hoping to return to a more healthful, humane way of eating soon. For now, survival, in a raw sense, motivates.

I flip through the books and review pictures of babies at the same stage of development as my own. How it should be looking at 10 weeks, how it will look at 12 . . . the relative size of the baby's hand throughout the nine months. But I still look for more information on the nausea. I find a little, but I'm already feeling the discomfort of faint perspiration and beginning undulations in my stomach.

Two books state: Morning sickness can be in your head. I almost wanted to throw up on the pages and stick in a note, "Don't worry about this apparent mess . . . it's all in your mind." Other books have explained, chemically, why pregnancy can result in nausea. They make some sense. This comment feels like a sexist insult. But a few sentences stick in my mind. Women in different cultures, the book said, literally experience early pregnancy differently. Nausea in pregnant women is common in America. Margaret Mead found that women in certain cultures never get nauseous, but have *boils*. They also *expect* to get boils when first pregnant. This is interesting. I've always been fascinated by the possibilities of mind over matter. I've certainly heard of women who weren't trying to get pregnant passing through the first few months noticing little unusual except a bit of fatigue and missed periods. An unmarried friend of mine who got pregnant unintentionally told me she had no problems at all in the beginning but did have difficulties at the end. Can I will this stuff away? God, I hope so, but there's not much time left for an empirical study. It's due to disappear soon anyway.

In my second pregnancy—nine weeks' worth, apparently dead at five weeks—I don't think I felt much nausea at all. This would go along with a physical cause. And the first time, I was sick (mostly throughout) although not as badly as this time. Books say mothers of twins usually experience more severe symptoms throughout pregnancy, including increased nausea the first trimester. And, since it's rare to know you're carrying multiples that early, to psych yourself into extra bouts with the toilet bowl seems unreasonable.

Perhaps this is one, too, we'll never know the answer to.

February 25

Sleeping. I have always loved sleeping late, but recently I seem to be elevating it to a high art form. I enjoy it while I'm at it, but the guilt is increasing. I'm embarrassed. I confess to few how late I rise. I can vow to get up earlier, but snuggling down in the morning has become the physical high point of my day. Comfort. No nausea.

I know it's not uncommon to need extra sleep. When I was working last year with the first pregnancy, I'd get up as late as possible in the morning and crash after work with a nap from six to nine. If Rick hadn't made me get up for dinner, I probably would have slept until morning.

Now, in a situation where I don't have to do anything, I don't do anything. My mother has always said I'm too hard on myself. So now and then, I try to remember to be kind to myself. What do I do with my time besides sleep? I've continued swimming, usually making it three times per week. My time in the water now ranges from 15 minutes to half an hour. This depends much less on fatigue than on when I get there. Too close to the end of lap swim and I only get 15 minutes. Also, I read. No great works, just magazine reading, a Scott Turow murder thriller (*Presumed Innocent*) and a Margaret Atwood novel (*Lady Oracle*) which is wonderfully amusing. Billed as a story of a writer who fakes her own death to start anew (am I so depressed that I'm drawn to such a book jacket?), it's much more, and very funny. I also reread Barbara Gorden's *Defects of the Heart*—light fiction with a plot based on the exposure of a teratogenic drug, a toxin, given in this case for miscarriages, which causes severe birth defects. God! And I even knew what this was about! I should probably stick to murder mysteries.

What else? I can pat myself on the back for things I don't do. I don't watch daytime TV. I never really have, although I am hooked on some nighttime soaps ("L.A. Law," "St. Elsewhere," "A Year in the Life," "thirtysomething" . . . even "Dallas" and "Falconcrest" on occasion, though they rank lower on my list). Sometimes I think I should get hooked on some morning show, to get me out of bed, but daytime television was always verboten during my formative years, and the prejudice has stuck. Only when I was home from school sick was such drivel permitted, and then at bedside. Vacation days did not count. Saturday morning viewing was permitted, but that too was curtailed at some point. Limits were put on evening television on school nights. How I hated it, and how unfair I thought it. Now I'm grateful and plan to instill similar house rules . . . if we ever get little beings to form and guide.

What else do I do? I'm working on this journal. It doesn't feel like something (yet), but I'd like it to be. What would I like it to be? What do I hope to find by writing it? Part of me uses it like a talisman or bargaining chip with God: I'll just keep writing, work through the past pain and loss, the uncertainty of the future, and you'll produce a happy, healthy baby. It will have a happy ending. Another part of me grips it, pointing me toward archiving the pains of the past year, to prepare me for the worst this time. It's going to happen again. I must be as ready as I can, because the third time is going to be even harder. I will have a vehicle, a life boat, to help me handle it. I will share the unsharable. And a third part of me, an evil cynical part, laughs at that. I lose the baby, I share some tears with the pages, and the project crumbles up. And what about the whole me? The sum of all those parts? I don't know. I write because writing has always helped me during hard times. I write to find out who I am.

Who I am is a big question these days.

The birds empty the feeder of sunflower seeds within two days. And I feel sure there are no squirrels helping, amazingly enough. It seems the male cardinal may have some competition. The female has been totally out of sight today but a second male, perhaps a tad smaller but as fiery red and crisp looking as his foe, has appeared on the perimeter. I think he's come to the feeder for some seeds, but I can't tell them apart yet. All I know is that one male keeps dive-bombing the other. One seems to perch on the trees on the right side of the house, the other on the left. I believe the established cardinals live on the left.

February 26

I'm almost a week late giving the dogs their monthly heartworm pill. The red reminder heart covers most of Monday's calendar square, and the calendar sits right there next to the telephone, and today is already Friday. The key to this failure is the desire to feed them the pills with their dinners — that's when I forget.

I'm hoping some passing time, maybe another half an hour, will help my system settle down. A bowl of cereal with sliced apple has put my gut in a wary place. I think it's gas, it's not yet full-blown nausea. I'm becoming more convinced that milk is giving me a problem, but I still insist on eating cereal. Stupidity? Lack of creativity with food? *Stubbornness*? Perhaps a refusal to acknowledge that yet something else is changing. Yet something else — a small, piddly thing — is out of my control. If my stomach settles down a bit, I will head for the pool. Friday afternoon is open swim, with three lap lanes available.

The daffodils planted in late November have begun pushing their heads through. By the time they bloom, two to three weeks I estimate, I should be blooming too. I'll be into the second trimester, energy should return, the days will be growing warmer, the bird's songs will increase, and the front woods should be glowing with a profusion of yellow and gold. So much needs to be done around the house and grounds! A small kernel of faith does exist in my soul. The few weeks left in this trimester will pass and I will be released. My writing teacher, in a continuing education class at Duke last year, described her first trimester to me: "It was like a great big elephant just came and sat on my chest for three months." Well, let's get this elephant going!

Swimming was good, except I guess my eating schedule was off. After throwing up the crackers I ate to calm my milk-laden stomach, I took off, only to heave in the toilets on an empty stomach after my hair was dried and I was almost dressed. Food has now helped a little.

What do you do with a 50-pound basset hound who's convinced she's a lap dog? Rub her ears and try and send her on her way.

Today I received some material heralding my tenth college reunion. I didn't go to the five-year meeting, and I am undecided about now. Poughkeepsie, New York is many miles away, but early June would be a good comfortable time in pregnancy to travel. Enclosed in the materials is a brief questionnaire for the catch-up bulletin that will be published a few weeks before the reunion. Some standard questions of address, marital status, kids, etc. And a kicker. "What have been the highlights of the past 10 years?" I suppose it's better than a 50th reunion . . . "What have been the highlights of your life?" Now, at least, if you're not sure or not satisfied, you have time to change, to hope, to do something about it. Five years out is no big deal. Many of us had barely begun life by then anyway, only recently out of graduate training. Not a lot is expected in the first five years. But 10 years. That is clearly enough time to do something, to have set your course, begun your path, made a mark as a rising young star. That is something about Vassar; ever so subtly it instills a belief or an expectation that you are important, that you are a doer. Not better than others, but not one who settles. Actually, I don't know whether the school instills that or whether the students bring it with them. Most, although frequently in unspectacular ways, are or become leaders of a type. Not necessarily with a string of achievements or a 20-page curriculum vita (although that is common), but in daily living. These women and men are capable and contribute.

After drafting a response to the highlights-of-the-last-10-years question, I realize I am not dissatisfied. I have not forged a clear-cut career, not climbed any identifiable ladder, but to date I am fairly satisfied. I've done a variety of things since schooling, with the faintest shadow of a common underpinning: writing. I am proud of being happily married but certainly not because being married is a preferred state of being; the status is not the fulfillment. Living alone is a challenge and a satisfaction of so many parts of oneself. But I am proud of being married because the daily act of being together is not easy. It is a different type of challenge to remember to give and take, to share, to accept a state of dependence without sacrificing other levels of independence. You learn different things about yourself when you live with another person so intimately. Perhaps it is the mutual nurturing of the relationship I value more than marriage. The legal knot became important to me, as much as I feared it, because I wanted to tell the world how important this other person was to me, how important I am to him. Having children comes in under similar thoughts and emotions. Not reasons, mind you. I believe it is the rational side of me that is scared to death. It is the emotions that have drawn a distinction about adoption that I never understood before now. Growing up, I always thought it was stupid to actually have your own children, or at least selfish. With all the unwanted children in the world, I didn't understand why everyone didn't adopt unless the kids were an accident.

Now I'm certainly not against adoption. And I've said, rather lightly, if we can't have our own children, we'll adopt. And while I know much of what makes a child, a person, is the love and care and guidance given by the parents, those raising it . . . while I know all this, I've learned I would feel devastated if we, in fact, can't have children. Why? It's not rational. That I know. But I want a being that is, literally, from Rick and me. Its raw material is us. And it's not the egoist part of wanting a little *me* running around—I pray daily the kid will be more like Rick—but wanting to celebrate to the world how much we love and respect each other. That *this* is the person each of us wants to create a future generation with, hoping, ridiculously, that the flaws on each side might get left out, and all the good stuff might get in.

When will I be able to write about the first miscarriage? And then the second. And then, ultimately, the Parent Care group for those grieving?

Soon.

February 29

"You're definitely miscarrying," the nurse said. I was there for my routine 12 week examination. The exams were conducted in a clinic at the hospital; it was large and crowded but I didn't have to wait too long. The nurse called me back. "Your progesterone is falling." As I stared at her with incomprehension, shock, she added, "It's supposed to go up. You're miscarrying."

She was so definitive. Was she suggesting a D&C? That was ridiculous. "But I talked to the doctor about it. 18.9. He said that was close enough, as long as the cramps stopped. And they have."

The nurse shook her head firmly. "It's going down. It's supposed to go up. You're not having any baby."

I was struck mute. I could barely speak, literally. My voice was hoarse, inaudible, forced from some spot deep within me. I was shaking. Terrified. "You don't understand," I forced, "this is my third pregnancy. I can't lose it."

The nurses bustled about eyeing each other knowingly, eyeing me warily. "It's natural to be depressed," one ventured.

"Yes, I know," I croaked, "I don't think I can handle this. I really can't. There must be a baby. The ultrasound saw the heartbeat." My voice was an agonizingly slow whisper. I could barely get anything out.

The nurse began discussing psychiatric help for me but I felt that was irrelevant. I wanted to save my baby. I was sure it wasn't too late. Just give me a shot of progesterone. Do an ultrasound to see.

"I'm not spotting," I said slowly, interrupting the nurse. "Or cramping." She sighed and turned away. "Is Dr. Fried here? What doctor is here? Call him please."

I had to reach Rick, too. He hadn't come to this appointment. I had to get him here to help me. I couldn't bear it if she was right. I asked for the phone but couldn't seem to get his number right. I was shaking. The nurses were still talking, rather cynically, about depression and psychiatric help. They had located Dr. Fried in the hospital, though, and said he'd be down after he finished delivering a baby.

I woke from this dream with my throat constricted and my voice slightly hoarse. I checked the sheets, I checked myself. No blood. My breasts are still tender but my nausea seems to have been receding a little over the last two days. (I have discovered a new helper, though, peppermint.)

The dream was so real. I slept again for a few more hours and shook the fear invading my body.

How would I deal with a third miscarriage, a third "spontaneous abortion"? The magical number that would transform me to a "habitual aborter." (Medical terminology is so reassuring.) I've been priming my psyche for this since the second one. Would I be matter-of-fact? Fall into a complete depression? Never rising. Never getting dressed. Never cleaning up, me or the house. Would I give up on pregnancy? It's a pretty raw deal, having to go through three first trimesters with not even one baby to show for it. Would I give up on kids completely? Rejecting adoption and following a childless life, devoting our love to each other, the dogs, our careers? Our legacies would be in our accomplishments, not in our children. I know Rick wants kids. Childless by choice would probably not be his option. I would probably have to do a lot of hard thinking myself with a year's sabbatical, at least, on any decision making about children.

What of the real ones, the real miscarriages?

The first, in a detached, quasi-scientific sense, was the most interesting. Perhaps I have to go through the mechanics of the event before I can explore and exorcise the pain.

I was visiting the doctors for a checkup at about 11 weeks. I'd elected coverage by their midwives. I was meeting the second one that day. I no longer remember her name. Rick was with me. The internal exam was fine; my uterus seemed in the ballpark of proper size. Then she brought out this little gizmo like an amplified stethoscope. It was to listen to the baby's heartbeat, she said. We could hear a lot of static and something of a rhythmic swoosh. But she explained that was only my blood pulsing. She listened hard and tried to find it for a long time. She explained she was a little concerned but not alarmed. The heart is normally audible at this point but my uterus is tipped (backwards). It points to the small of my back rather than toward my abdomen. I've known this for many years and have been told it's of no consequence; it's like being left-handed. Sometimes it just happens. The only disadvantage, I've learned through pregnancies, is that it's harder to examine in the early months. When the baby is big enough, the uterus expands upward, like all uteri.

So, the midwife explained, it was probably not a big deal. She confirmed I'd had no cramping or spotting. Then she outlined the options: we could wait two weeks and come back again to let her listen or we could get an ultrasound to see how everything looked right now. She was still fairly reassuring. Rick and I (still so innocent) were calm but decided we didn't want to fret about it for two weeks. The ultrasound was scheduled for that afternoon. Rick had to go back to work. He'd only been at the job four months.

On my own, my nerves let loose. I only had a few hours to wait. I went back to work, not concentrating, attending the first hour of a meeting, and forcing down glasses of water. The test needed a full bladder. I couldn't tell anyone. All I could say was that I had to go back to the doctor's that afternoon for another test, but they didn't think it was serious. They knew I was nervous, but they respected my obvious omissions as to what doctor, what test, what problem. I was a little excited, too. OK, I'd see the baby's heartbeat, and we'd know everything was fine.

The ultrasound test was at another office. They also conducted radiology tests there, so the waiting room was filled with an assortment of people, many older and looking ill, some children. I didn't see any obviously pregnant women. My bladder was aching. I later learned the eight glasses of water I needed amount to eight six-ounce cups, not eight 10-ounce glasses, as I'd consumed. I had to wait almost an hour before I was actually on the table. The worker was nice but ultimately didn't say much. If I'd known more, known how the technicians normally tell you exactly what they're looking at, I would have been frightened. But I wasn't. I was just a little nervous.

The technician spread conducting jelly on the instrument she'd press along my lower abdomen, seeking an image on her shades-of-grey computer screen. She told me my bladder was nice and full (as if I didn't know) and told me my tipped uterus made ultrasounds much more difficult to read. Were we to be stuck in ambiguity land anyway, I wondered? She took a long time (probably 20 minutes) which again, had I known, might have scared me. When things are OK, even on me, I now know one can be read in about five minutes.

I asked her some questions about what she saw, and somehow she both answered me and deflected me. I didn't know it then. She took several plates. The doctor in that office would read them and call over to my doctor's office. I was to go back there, and they'd talk to me. This did not sound good.

I emptied my bladder with a gush of relief I'd never felt before, dressed, and drove around the block to the OB-GYN office. I had only a short wait this time. The midwife led me back.

How I wanted to tell this story! To relive it and put it to bed! But, right now, I just can't.

March 29

The crucial month. *A* crucial month? March is over. I'm 15 weeks pregnant.

I couldn't do it. I got right up to the nitty gritty of remembrance and review, and I clutched. I choked. Silently. I put down my pen. I couldn't even chronicle this month.

I will finish my story. But how to catch up on the last month? It's gone much faster than any of the earlier *weeks*. Gradually, at no specified point, I stopped counting the days that would inch me along to another week. Gradually I stopped staring at my panties and the toilet paper for telltale spotting. I still look, I realize. I may well keep looking until there's a baby in my arms, but there's less fear. It's less conscious. I'm still nauseous off and on. I'm still throwing up. The intensity is easing up, the constancy.

When we visited the doctor for a 12-week checkup in early March, he heard the heartbeat. Rick could hear it, too. I couldn't distinguish it from my own. I expected to feel a wave of relief at that time. It was the farthest along I'd ever been and the baby was definitely alive. But I didn't. For a while I was more depressed than ever. I wrestled with it. Was I depressed at having a child after all? Did I really not want one? Then the depression compounded with insidious guilt. If that was true, did I somehow reject my own first two pregnancies, abort them because underneath it all I didn't want them? Those thoughts were too horrible to handle head-on at the time. Maybe I was just depressed because of my hormones. I knew they weren't helping my equilibrium.

Anger, too, invaded my soul. Anger at my body for fooling me again, for giving me hope (clear hope) when assuredly it would only betray me again. I dared hope two times before. I tried to learn. I tried not to hope at all. I succeeded very well through most of the first trimester. I didn't feel warm and cuddly toward the contents of my womb. I felt nothing. Or I felt anger. All this physical upheaval and unpleasantness and interference with my goals was for naught. There will be no purpose except loss and pain. And then depression. Anger turned inward because anger is not an appropriate emotion at this time.

Where or when all this began to give way I'm not sure. Somewhere in the last three weeks. During this past month I went to a maternity clothes shop for the first time. I felt self-conscious. I don't look pregnant yet although most of my pants are too tight. I'm foraging among Rick's shirts, and my breasts have been screaming out for months for super-support bras. But with a wedding to attend in April, at about 20 weeks, I knew I owned nothing appropriate.

The store had few formal dresses, but my hour-long venture turned from a self-conscious embarrassment of "I don't belong in here" to almost giddy glee as an obviously happy and committed saleswoman brought me more bathing suits, shorts, tops, and bras. I wound up leaving with two pairs of shorts, one summer top, a denim skirt, and a new bra in a startling 36D. For most of my life, I've considered myself small breasted, wearing foam-enhanced bras in junior high and high school. I haven't done that since, but I've never thought of myself as a large-breasted woman. Now, when I get out of bed I have to hold up my breasts to keep the pain of gravity away for a while. It's downright bizarre.

How else have I quietly affirmed the fact that I'm pregnant? I joined a prenatal exercise class at the Y. Everyone in there is due relatively soon but other barely-starteds are likely to join. Most of these women have been going for a long time. The warmer weather has me decorating the house, mostly framing and hanging our pictures, but also getting a few more plants and looking for a quilt to hang in the large empty space above the foyer. I still tire easily but I have much more energy.

The daffodils I planted in the fall have blossomed and look wonderful. I'd like to keep flowers there among the rocks and the trees throughout the summer. We'll see.

April 8

I heard the baby's heartbeat today for the first time! I heard it! Of course, so did Rick and Linda (one of our two midwives). I just lay there grinning. It was great. And though I couldn't *feel* it, the baby kept moving around! Amazing! We'd have to chase after it to find the heartbeat again. And Rick and I felt how far up my uterus has grown. By next month (20 weeks) it should be as high as my navel! I think I feel convinced for the first time there's a baby in there. I can hardly wait to feel it move. An I feel so healthy psychologically. What I mean is that I feel affirmed, inside, by external signs that my body and baby are doing great.

Baby's heart rate came in at 144, the normal range being 120 to 160. My blood pressure is low (90 over 50). My hematocrit (iron count) is up from 37 last month to 43! No protein or sugar is passing in my urine. My uterus is just at the height it should be (halfway to the navel). And the little baby is, literally, alive and kicking. Yippee!! I'm not just *sitting here*, I'm actually producing something!

Linda wants me to gain four pounds by next month.

I feel great! The vitamins (as of Monday) are now staying down and sitting fine. I've been exercising four times per week. I'm doing OK!

April 21

I felt the first flutters, like a few pea-size bubbles inside. But there! If the tales are true and delivery is five months after the first movement is felt, I'll be right on my due date.

April 26

I've been feeling them all week, usually when I'm quiet and relaxing. But today I felt one significantly more pronounced while waiting to check folks into classes at the Arts Center.

April 29

Last night, while lying down in bed, I felt a series of movements. Now, though still faint or light, they aren't exactly bubbles. I grabbed Rick's hand and put it on my abdomen, fingers splayed to cover as much space as possible. Sort of waiting for a pot to boil. The baby goes on motion strike if we want the baby to move. But he felt one! One that I thought was rather faint. He said it was like a little wave, and that does best describe it now.

I've been busy this month. Not feeling I've accomplished much in terms of tasks and goals, but busy. With what? Swimming and exercise class and walks with Mara. The Duke class ("Psyche in Search of the Ancient Goddess"). Arts Center volunteering. I don't know what else is filling it, what with all I *want* to do.

I took a trip with Kim yesterday to examine baby gear. She's the wife of a friend of Rick's. She's also the mother of one-year-old triplets. I think she liked looking at baby clothes a little better than cribs, changing tables, and car seats. I don't get excited about baby clothes, but I feel a strong need to purchase all necessary equipment.

May 4

I continue to be delighted with Pony's movements. I still think of it/him/her more often as "the baby," but "Pony" is also somehow fitting. Rick has started to refer to the little one as Pony. I don't think either of us know exactly how that nickname evolved.

I was touched Saturday by a birthday gift memorializing this special time. Rick found a tiny ceramic pony — rounded and toylike in appearance — a rocking horse with a small, pale blue patch on its rear and a pink flower over its tail. The lack of realism in its representation made it all the more endearing since we're obviously not talking about a *horse* anyway!

I find other mothers' comments interesting. A woman I barely know called today about some business regarding the Newcomers Club (with which I've been peripherally involved). First, after inquiring about my current state of pregnancy, she complimented me, saying I looked the picture of health at the last dinner meeting. That felt nice, as at the time I was still feeling lousy. Then she laughed (not meanly) and said "We'll see how long that lasts!" Realizing her faux pas, she tried to backtrack and said, "Well, I mean after a few years . . . " and (realizing that wasn't really any better) added, " . . . 10 years! Kids can really take it out of you," she finished lamely. I laughed and just said I thanked my lucky stars that my stomach was back to normal and moved on.

Thunder has been rumbling this afternoon through the humidity. It rained in spurts, as the clouds part now and again for weak sunshine. And the waters pour down again, rushing through the leaves, darting across the cedar shingle roof. The trees have grown so thick that the road is invisible, only one patch peeks through by the corner of the fence. And I thought the leaves were out when the daffodils and redbud and azaleas were blooming last month! The first spring at this house — how much we learn through time.

I'm becoming more interested in planting a tree somewhere in the yard at the birth of this child. If fall is a bad time to plant, then within its first year. I'd like to plant something that flowers.

One distant yet long continuous rumble backs the increasing crescendo of rainfall. The water slows, punctuated again by thunder.

The class at Duke, within Continuing Education, has fascinated me for the last five weeks. All of us attending are sorry it's ending next week. We talk of continued meeting on our own. "Psyche in Search of the Ancient Goddess" is a mouthful of a title that always needs an explanation. Applying the ancient mythology of goddesses and goddess worship to ourselves, our culture today. Feminist psychology. I feel more in tune with these women — and on many levels we are widely divergent — than any other group with which I'm currently in contact. More than at the Arts Center, more than at prenatal exercise class. The books that are mentioned, the discussions, the sharing of dreams and fantasy/relaxation work in class, the discussions on menstruation: all were wonderful. Today K.K. reported that when doing her homework — discussing the topic of menstruation with someone outside the class — her friend gave her an incredulous look, saying, "And you *paid* for this class?" and promptly changed the subject. Why are people afraid of this? And what is *this* anyway? I don't mean simply discussing menstruation, I mean challenging the status quo. So many people today (even female contemporaries!) see feminism as something trendy in the '60s and '70s. "It made its point," or "we have what we need," or "it got us into trouble" — pick your poison. A continuation of historic struggle, feminism hardly *started* in the 1960s! While the goddess class is not a history of feminism, it opens doors to the female presence in ancient history.

Our introductory text, Jean Shinoda Bolen's *Goddesses in Everywoman*, moved my mind in interesting directions. For most of my adult life I suppose I've seen myself as an Artemis or Athena: strong, independent, comfortable in the male world when I chose to enter it, and childless. I have even harbored prejudice against mothers! I had a sense of women being one or the other, mother or professional, with little vision of productive (nonburnout) overlap. Mothers (my internal emotional stereotype went) were relentlessly other-focused and immersed in a world with a small cast of characters.

How can I be a Demeter or a Hestia, getting all joy out of hearth, home and babe? That's not who I am! The class readings have, on some levels, heightened my identity crisis. Yet they have bolstered me. Women need not be only one or the other; the fluidity of our psyches and our lives is to be applauded. Whether it's one goddess then another (giving form to our lives in sequence) or several at once (balancing each other day by day) we need not be compartmentalized. I know I've always looked forward to being a wise old woman, and now I've learned there was once a name for that valued position: the Crone! Only lately has patriarchy successfully changed the emotional charge associated with that age and status. Too bad. Maybe I can bring back the beauty of being a hag. But that's so far away! First I must adjust to and thrive in my middle "Queen" years — and as a Mommy Queen to boot!

Three body-long sneezes in rapid succession from the basset. She grinds her nose into the carpet, by my feet, now apparently having appeased the itch. Using her doggie instincts, she paws away at the rug, making a nest before she sits, then collapses completely.

As Pony moves now and again in the day and more noticeably as I read in bed at night, my life is so full. I find satisfaction from little things. After two or three weeks of planning and thinking (i.e., procrastination), I finally converted three pairs of regular pants into maternity pants. The process is irreversible, so it was tough selecting which pants to transform. The life span will be short, so not the ones of which I'm most fond. Yet I want to feel good, so I don't want to be wearing the rejects I haven't yet given away or thrown out. I finally compromised: one pair I've loved and worn a lot but which are reaching their last legs; one pair I like but which were too snug before pregnancy; and one pair that is functional, but too short, so not my favorite. But at last the task is done, my wardrobe enlarged, and my waist more comfortable!

Although the thunder has stopped, both pups are settled in the wide center cave of my desk. The action is up here (i.e., me), so now they are here, too. Feeling calm and centered, with the rain and the dogs for company, I'm ready to return to the memory of the first miscarriage.

I had undergone the ultrasound and returned to the doctor's office. The wait was brief. A few patients were seated on the pale peach and muted green and blue furniture. Regardless, I was first. They didn't leave me out there long. The midwife led me back to her office. She gently explained, with a hint of a tear in her eye and a catch in her throat, that I shouldn't get my hopes up. I would probably start bleeding and cramping that weekend and miscarry. I should call the office when it happened. Although the ultrasound was slightly ambiguous, it appeared the baby had stopped growing at around nine weeks. And they could see no heartbeat. Wasn't my husband with me? Did I want her to call him?

I nodded. I choked back my tears. I was not going to wail in this office. I was not going to cry because there was still a fragment of hope. Her prediction might not be true. My tipped uterus could be deceiving them. The operator might be unskilled. I felt fine! Rufus (our pet name for the first baby) might be hiding, camera shy. We tried to laugh a few days later when my spotless panties and cramp-free uterus allowed us to hope a little more. It was Thursday when the test was done, February 5th. I was 11 1/2 weeks pregnant. I believe I talked to my mother that night, but soon after the meeting with the midwife, I began to suppress, to cling more openly to hope. At work, a haze. I was tense, remembered little. It was, I believe, harder to be optimistic when no one there knew about the baby in the first place.

I found some solace and a life raft in the woman who worked across the hall. Shirl, a mother of eight grown children, was the ample and loving mother I needed. Behind closed doors that week, I told her the truth: the pregnancy, the ultrasound, the ambiguity, the waiting. She hugged me and held me and gave me what I needed, a presence. A knower of my hopes and anguish, my excitement and terror.

The following Thursday morning (February 12th) at work, the ladies room. The palest, faintest, pinkish-tan line appeared on my panties, echoing mildly on the toilet tissue. I froze. As on the night my father died more than 10 years before, everything assumed a heightened clarity. Brilliant and brittle. My mind was paradoxically clear and functional, logical and aware, yet incapable of moving forward.

Portions of my readings and the comments by the midwives and nurses stayed sharply in my mind. "Spotting is fairly common, it doesn't necessarily mean anything." I still would not acknowledge reality. Of course I called Rick immediately and tearfully told Shirl, but I inside I wouldn't give up. I wasn't cramping. I'd never seen such light spotting. I was still pregnant. I stayed at work. (Other written wisdom had said if you're going to miscarry, you'll do so regardless of your activities.)

By the end of the work day, the bleeding had increased only slightly. I had also called the midwives and was instructed to do what I felt like doing and to call back when or if the bleeding or cramping grew heavy. Somewhere along the line, I had asked and been told I could stay home through it if I wanted to. A D&C might not be necessary. And I knew I should save the tissue. I knew that, if I could, I would rather handle a miscarriage at home and not have a D&C if it could be avoided. When Rick came home, we were cautious, neither optimistic nor pessimistic for those interim hours. I have no memory of dinner that night. We were frozen in time. I was wearing a sanitary pad by then.

Around 7:30 or 8:00 p.m., we were watching T.V. I felt a gush and knew it was over. I thought I was finally bleeding. I went upstairs to change and was startled to discover that, although the bleeding had increased some, the rush had been the breaking of my water, an event associated with *birth*. I never even gave much thought to the amniotic sac. Its destruction made me very sad. It seemed a concrete way of saying "There was a *baby* in there, and you're about to lose it."

Almost immediately afterward I passed my first clot. At the time, I thought that was it—the tissue, the fetus, whatever. It was about 1″ × 1″ and deep dark red. The lining. (A piece of it.) Yet, then, I had incomplete knowledge of miscarriages. I asked Rick, dubiously, if he wanted to see it. He did. Like me, he concluded it wasn't so bad. A fresh pad, more blood, and more clots. I called the doctors and was called back quickly. Yes, if I felt like staying at home, that was OK. No tampons. (Infection, I knew that.) If I began bleeding heavily or passed clots larger than a half-dollar, call back. An hour later I was passing clots bigger than a half-dollar. The call back was fruitless; I didn't have to go to the hospital unless I wanted to go. (If I did, I'd get a D&C to shorten and allegedly neaten up the event.)

I stayed home. I'd do it that way again (I did), but I'm still surprised by the ease with which I handled the crisis, dealt with the mess. Every 15 minutes or half hour, I was in the bathroom wrapping a new superabsorbent Kotex with "wings" around my panty. They were each soaked to their plastic liners. I could feel the gentle glide every time another clot slid from my body. Like a detached medical technician I scooped each into the pale yellow plastic storage container. An old butter dish, useful for leftovers, extra tuna fish, dog stools to the vet, and, now, uterine linings.

Rick stayed up with me. With the rapid, constant flow, I didn't see how I could go to bed yet. At times, the clots were almost as large as my fist. Yet the physical pain was merely discomfort. Until later.

By 1:00 a.m. it seemed to be slowing. I collected about four towels to line my side of the bed, and I took a long hot shower. The blood continued to drip to the shower floor. I suddenly realized I was dizzy. I didn't know whether from loss of blood, fatigue, or, now, fear. It began to hurt. Had I been stupid to stay home? Was I hemorrhaging? I didn't know.

I crawled into bed at 1:45. Rick had fallen asleep. I, too, was exhausted. Even in sleep he reached out and held my hand. By 2:00 I was in agony. True cramps. Strong contractions. I wasn't sure what was going on. I thought about going to the hospital. I tried to breath deeply and slowly. Apparently I was moaning. I guess I knew it, yet didn't know it was audible. Rick was awake. What could he do? What should he do? After months of avoiding all medication, not wanting to risk even possible damage to a baby while trying to conceive — after months, I decided some Extra-Strength Tylenol might help. 2:15. Rick brought it to me. "Should we go to the hospital?" I asked. Rick soothed me. Apparently, I had communicated my strength through the evening better than I was communicating my fear of the moment. We lay in the dark as I clutched his hand, curling my knees to my chest in the near constant pain; 2:30 was the last I saw the clock as the pain eased and I fell asleep.

I woke around 7:00. As I got up, I felt something between my legs. In the bathroom I realized *this* must be the tissue. It was tan colored. I knew it was the placenta. Part of it was long, twisted, and tough, like the cord. I didn't have the heart to examine it in any depth, I just added it to the butter dish. I was only spotting now —

red — but very light. There was no pain. None of any sort. I was numb. Rick too.

I called work early enough to get the machine. I couldn't talk to anyone. Friday. I wouldn't be able to come in that day. I knew Shirl had left town the day before because one of her daughters was in labor prematurely. Her daughter had been working on having a baby 11 years, had had several later miscarriages, and was diagnosed as having an incompetent cervix. She'd been sewn up in the fall. Now the baby wanted to come almost three months early. He was named Matthew. So, with Shirl gone, I didn't know how anyone would know about me.

But Friday morning. We were at the doctor's by 8:30 and seen promptly. The doctor examined me. He lifted the placenta from the dish, examined it quickly, and told us it looked like the abortion was complete. He was kind and gentle. He was reassuring yet aware he shouldn't try to minimize our pain.

A nurse asked us if we wanted to keep the contents of the butter dish. I think we said "no" quickly and asked her why anyone would. She seemed uncomfortable but said some people wanted to bury it or plant a tree. Later, I wished we hadn't been so quick to decide. The nurse should be applauded for asking. I fervently hope my reaction didn't discourage her from asking someone else. I can only think I was still operating in my medical mentality. I have one, I know. At 12 I was a whiz at dissecting earthworms. At 15 I taxidermied a mouse with aplomb. And, at 29, I collected my fetus, with numb efficiency, I guess.

Another nurse gave me my shot of RhoGAM in the butt. I had already told the first nurse and the doctor. I didn't want it forgotten. I'm Rh − and Rick's Rh + . . . I know the preventive need.

We went home, stopping at Shoneys for breakfast, unable to believe it was over. The pregnancy, our first baby, was aborted. Spontaneously aborted.

May 5

The aftermath of those 24 hours is far foggier than the event itself.

In the midst of the miscarriage that Thursday night, my brother Rob called to see how I was doing. I made it short, telling him through tears that I was miscarrying. He sounded genuinely upset. Saturday a lovely flower arrangement arrived. His note was to the effect that he hoped I'd be better soon, but the fact of flowers was affirmation of the death of our baby. Baby to be. Since we never named it, beyond the playful Rufus, I have still not yet adjusted to or defined the status of either miscarriage. Loss of a *potential* or loss of a *baby*? My views of freedom of choice for abortion push me hard to keep it potential—a real, viable potential—but no baby I could see yet. This contrasts radically with what I feel and believe now at 20 weeks. I feel this *baby move* inside me. Even though it is still too young to ever survive outside my body, it feels like a living baby.

It's funny. When I talked to Peter, my other brother, on Sunday and told him that I'd felt the baby move, he was pleased and interested but asked an odd question. He seemed puzzled and asked if I felt it move by putting my hands on my abdomen. It seemed alien or unthinkable to him that I felt the movement on the inside, from the inside, as if he's never considered that!

And Rob, I talked to him this week, too. When I was so excited about feeling the baby, he was excited too but so cautious. He asked if we felt safer now, if it *was* safer now, more certain. I know we discussed this at around 12 weeks and I felt a little more secure then, but it seems Rob has been holding back, not yet ready to believe he'll actually be an uncle. He was surprised that 20 weeks was halfway there. I felt hurt that he seemed to be denying the pregnancy. That's a totally inaccurate description of his words, I know. At worst, he's only protecting himself. Perhaps my hurt was more a recognition of a ripple of fear, the remembrance (on a visceral level) that there are no guarantees. About anything. Ever.

So the question still nags: How can you ever get excited or hopeful about anything? Maybe I've found my own answer, as I am clearly excited about Pony. Has the act of creation alone provided that hope, the embracing of life? Is it growth and maturation, healing through time? What a boring answer. Everyone is told, "Time heals all." At the brink, you have such doubts that you can even stand there and let time wash over you, much less try and move forward with it, through it. Somehow it includes learning to accept that pain will not annihilate you. It may temporarily cripple, but the evolving person gains new understanding. Permanently. Character building is the common view.

Is it a greater, clearer connection to the cyclical nature of all things? Certainly most make it through by communing with their God. I have always felt so handicapped there. Not pure atheist, but God has never been *my* God, nor anyone else's. An abstract and distant — what — thing? View? Entity? I never could say. Neither punishing nor kind, it just is. But too large to relate to in a personal sense. If it becomes personal, I just become argumentative and resentful. *What* larger plan? If you're so all-powerful, and I need to grow, why be so nasty as to cause such personal pain and to snuff a burgeoning new life? You're simply not a personal and intervening God, because if you are, you're a cruel one I cannot accept. That thinking goes far beyond my own personal little world. Learning about the Holocaust at a young age was a pretty illustrative example. The piles of bodies spoke louder than any doctrine or gospel. All wars and atrocities, bigotry and brutality, speak against a personal God.

Free will is a nice concept to throw into the intellectual morass, but it doesn't explain the death of babies. Babies who are loved and cared for with scrupulous attention. These babies, whose *will* is it for them to leave their families? No one's. Which is why I have no personal God.

Yet I'm not alienated from spirituality. It is a process I refine as I go, which keeps me connected to the day-to-day and to the universal. But it doesn't hold my hand. I don't know how it helps me. Frankly, I am not at all sure that it helps me through at all. I have no confidence it will be there for me in future tragedy. Keeping a shadow or trace memory of some exquisite pains of the past, I have no faith I could survive a tragedy too deep. This baby dying. Rick dying. I have always considered myself a strong person. I still do. But some things you fear deeply.

Yet through all this, I can still feel vibrant and alive and so curious about the little baby growing inside me.

A year ago February I lay on my bed, resting after the first miscarriage the previous night. I slept a little. I rested a great deal. I was immobile in my numbness. It was a sunny day. No snow on the ground in the Piedmont. I watched the sun play through the windows. Rick slept. I don't think he went to work that day, yet I remember so little. During the preceding week of denial and hope, I had quietly allowed a little common sense to prevail. I purchased a copy of *Coping With a Miscarriage* by Hank Pizer and Christine O'Brien Palinski.

My memory lies to me again. I picked it up Thursday, February 12, on the way home from work. The brittle medical clarity prevailed. I recall wondering, as I bought the book, if this person at the register had even the vaguest notion of what was happening to me. Small stains accumulating between my legs while I prepared to understand what was happening to me. As I rested, seeing the light play through the bedroom of our new house on Friday morning—an odd thing—I picked up the book. I read.

I learned much that morning. Touching base, through the pages, with another woman who had miscarried and learning scientific facts. What's known and what's unknown. I was to learn then, confirmed last May and again at the start of this pregnancy, that the world of medicine knows very little. A list of possible causes emerged. Chromosomal problems—both genetic abnormality (rare in relation to the number of miscarriages) and abnormality in the cell-splitting process of early conception (a common, random, genetic screwup). Other causes included uterine anatomic abnormalities, uterine adhesions, infections, chemical/environmental assault, autoimmune conditions, hormones, thyroid, diabetes, luteal phase inadequacy and endometriosis.

At the time, it seemed it might be easy to find the cause and make sure it was fixed. We were never able to locate any cause. We're stuck with assuming a random genetic defect, which is fine. Treatment is not necessary or even possible. Fine, except we're still left feeling helpless and powerless.

Friday was a quiet day. I had called Mom Thursday night. Brief. Tearful. For both of us. She offered to come down. I declined. She called me back Friday morning. More joint tears, yet the memory is gone. I asked her to talk to Pete. Rob already knew. Somehow, sometime, my aunt, uncle, and two cousins had to be told. As I'd been quick to impart the good news, they had to know there was no more baby. I couldn't do it myself. Friday night Rick started calling his family. I couldn't speak to anyone. My father-in-law and step-mother-in-law insisted on speaking to me, and I just burst into tears.

Rick and I talked and cried and hugged much of the evening. He was afraid it was his fault, as I was afraid it was my body that was defective. Yet I haven't suffered any guilt about anything I did. I was so damn careful and healthy that I could never come up with anything to blame. But my sweetheart told me what irrational fear was plaguing him (beyond worries of two-headed sperm). He feared God was punishing him. I could only stroke him and hold him and tell him it wasn't so.

The next day was Valentine's Day. We had each done our preparation early enough that we had our gifts and cards on hand. Such a bittersweet day. Professing our love as we grieved for the lost embodiment of that love.

I thought I was ready to return to work on Monday, but heavy snow and slick ice closed the city for most of the week. I stayed home knitting a baby blanket, of all things, watching afternoon TV, and reading. The first two activities were totally out of character for me. It was a time much like that Friday morning. A lot of sitting, quietly immobilized.

I was better when I went back to work. I cried at times and shared with a few others what had happened. Some gave me cards; Anna brought me a pot of pink hyacinths. Working with all women was quietly supportive although several months later, after the second miscarriage, I was ready to kill a sweet and well-meaning co-worker. That instance occurred near the end of a long involved staff meeting, wrangling with how to make the agency function better, meeting both client needs and our needs. Mary Kay pointed out the significance of job stress level—at least three miscarriages in the last five months. Another woman on our staff of 20 had miscarried (early and after years of infertility). She hadn't even known she was pregnant. (Somehow I'm convinced—wrongly I'm sure—that that lack of prior knowledge made it easier for her.) Anyway, Mary Kay felt people were miscarrying due to the stress of the jobs and that such stress levels were ridiculous.

I was furious and barely controlled. My words were brief. Although I was often frustrated with the agency, I was *not* stressed. Unlike others, I did not bring the clients' problems home with me. I did not accrue weeks and weeks of comp time. I knew healthy limits, and I set them. And I *bitterly* resented someone telling me (indirectly or no) that my job, my actions, caused my miscarriages. I knew it wasn't so, yet some of my fury must have fed on the fact that I could never truly know.

It was this fury, combined with several other irrational out-of-proportion reactions at home and at work, that led us in July to Parent Care. What else? A week on the Outer Banks with a close woman friend, with Rick joining for the last three days, did little to rejuvenate me. The week I got back I dissolved in tears with a woman under my supervision. She was reporting to me that other workers she supervised didn't like the way I handled something in her absence. The enormity of my reaction can only be understood in the context of who I am. I may be in touch with my emotions, but in a professional context, crying is totally alien to me. I didn't need any more signs. I called Parent Care.

May 13

A strange dream last night. But what's even stranger, given the dream, is that it wasn't disturbing in the slightest while I was having it. I only remember the core. It was time to have the baby, although I seemed not much bigger than now. Rick and I were with our midwife, Linda, in some hospital setting. The fact that we plan to have a natural childbirth didn't come up here.

Linda needed to operate. I was extremely neutral. More curious. Anesthesia wasn't part of the dream. I was wearing a blue hospital smock (the same cornflower blue as the maternity outfit I was wearing yesterday). She said she'd mark the spot with water marks on the gown, making a pattern. She dipped her hand into some water and started drawing on my tummy, beginning at the bottom. The wetness began to create a pattern on my stomach. I was interested.

Linda laughed easily and said she'd use the "devil pattern" since it was the most effective. At first the water marks seemed very general, with little form at all, but as she finished a very clear and rather artistic devil face or mask was apparent. She picked up a small instrument, almost like a dental probe. She held it over my tummy, pressing it momentarily into the point of the beard, and raised it again, readying to pierce through the hospital gown.

I was thoroughly calm. At that point a man standing near me, a combination of Rick and my father, asked incredulously, "Aren't you *scared*?"

"Don't ask me that!" I snapped and began to feel a small snake of fear as I woke up.

Listening to "The Best of Joan Baez," after musing on this dream, is uplifting: invigorating and moving bittersweet music. Old familiar songs I classify as folk songs.

I am at Elaine's for the week, my friend since the first month of law school. We'll head off to the beach today for most of the duration. The forecast predicts several days of drizzle. As long as it's not an incessant downpour, I'll be fine. I like walking and sensing the beach rather than pure sunning anyway. Especially these days when I'm wary of acquiring "the mask of pregnancy" (brown splotches that hang on until after the birth).

The fear I knew in early pregnancy, the fear that caused me to hesitate to make travel plans at all, has returned. Only in shadow form, but it's there. Of course, the night before I leave I experience some brand new abdominal twitches or cramps. Not painful, but noticeable. I joke with Elaine at the grocery store about picking up a box of Pampers just in case. But there is no "just in case." If my body were to release the baby now, little Pony would die. Pony, who kicks and squirms and makes his presence more apparent every day. Pony would die.

How I could stand it in any circumstance I don't know, but if anything should happen while I'm away from Rick and our own doctors, I don't know how I could live with it. It's so silly. Is it just loose free-form guilt looking for a home? It's certainly not logical. There is nothing in my activity that could cause a problem. Do I just feel guilty for having, and taking, the option of a good time? A vacation? A communion with a friend? A communion without my husband. I've done it before, and I intend to do it again, but perhaps the growing baby insists on painting a more traditional picture in my head. It spotlights that part of society that does not expect a wife and mother to travel alone, unless of course she's leaving, she's running, she's hiding a problem. Well, I know I'd be miserable in a stereotyped existence that buried my individuality, my self, but maybe it's the baggage of society that I carry reflecting itself in my fear of losing the baby while being independent. Maybe it's simply the insecurity and dependence that grows with the bulk of pregnancy. For as much of the process that is under the influence of my conduct and behavior, much more is totally out of my control. This baby and my body will do what they want to do. This basic helplessness is highlighted in the glow of my very self-controlled and decisive activity.

I can only be in charge, be willful, be creative, in so many aspects of my life. Sometimes life itself moves on its own, and one is only left to react as best as one can.

May 14

The beach! Free and flying through the whitened air and sand. The gulf has gentle ripples for waves, full of auditory rhythms of beach lullaby, but so tame there's nothing to fear.

I took a brisk 40-minute walk this morning before the sun was up too high. My thighs began to tingle and feel gelatinous (incredibly discouraging considering all the exercise I've been doing). I can only conclude that sand walking works different muscles than swimming, road walking, or prenatal exercise class.

It's 4:00 p.m. and I feel a lazy sleepiness creeping over me. My mind wants to read my novel (about a pregnant Southern woman whom I can't relate to) and I don't know which part of my being will win out.

May 15

My tears are just drying and I'm trying to convince myself it must be from my hormone level. For half an hour tears slid down my cheeks; I couldn't shake the shadow of intense loss and grief.

Something had happened to Rick or was about to happen. He was hurt. Or the unimaginable agony — he was dead. How could I possibly go on? All the intensity of my love for him welled up, filling the room, hitting the white sun filtering through the glass that surrounds me. Sharp light. Light of no comfort. I'm here, unreachable. Unable to help him, protect him. No one even able to find me to tell me (we have no telephone). It's as if I have some power when I'm there, home, when we're together. Some power to see him safe. To protect his life. The echo of such a reality playing uninvited across my mind tears me in two. I just want to go home. I want the week to be over so I can be with him.

My cheeks are dry again, and I try to analyze. Is there too much solitude here? At home I fight it by organizing my day with activities and errands. The days, recently, have been going quickly. But since my arrival in Florida, time seems to have slowed to a crawl. I know I react differently to a straight week of timeless freedom at the coast when I've escaped a nine-to-five work-a-day world. I revel in the freedom to read on end, the luxury of unimpeded, unmarked hours. But they seem so long now. So lonely. Elaine, with a hectic full-time work schedule, is recouping, I think, as I would under the circumstances. Yet I feel we're not talking much, connecting only now and then. We're on different schedules: when, or whether, to walk or swim, have a meal, wake up, or take a nap. We're both reading a lot which isn't the best activity to foster communication. I tend to avoid the sun in the hotter part of the day when she'll nap on the sand.

The beach, although white sand, is rugged. I see the evidence of a moving coast line, ravaged tree stumps in the water, barely standing from the continued wear of the waves. A few tall barren ghosts of life stand farther away, still surrounded by sand. The water is a murky brownish grey-green. Our house is so close to the water that, when gazing out from the living room, we appear to be floating in the sea. Yet the sky, the sand, the trees, the water — everything — is bleached. Stark. Unforgiving. Uncompromising. Unyielding. Lonely.

When has solitude ever left me feeling lonely? It has happened, I know, but more often it has refreshed me. It seems so many days until Saturday. And this yearning for home so perplexes me. I had looked forward to this trip for so long. Back home, I kept thinking how it would be the end of June before I could bat an eye: nine days with Elaine, then a long anniversary weekend with Rick on Kiawah, then (in only a week or two more) a week off with Nancy in Portland and the Pacific Northwest. Poof, it's June 15th!

We connected last night, talking for a long time after dinner. About pregnancy, birth, and life after baby. Elaine even felt Pony kick! It was a good talk, though I think it became a bit one-sided, as I did so much of the talking.

Maybe I'm in a funk from the change in routine. For the last six weeks, I've been going swimming twice a week, taking an exercise class twice a week, taking the course at Duke, and going to the Arts Center (often twice a week). I think time went quickly.

Maybe I'm again in the throes of waiting, not living. Whatever it is, I want to snap out of this funk.

May 17

That mood passed about as quickly as it descended. The light is still a harsh white, and the little green lizard is still making his noontime parade across the deck: a few quick steps, raise and bob the neck, inflate the red balloon under his chin, deflate, and dart along a few paces again. The sound of the waves has gradually worked its hypnotic serene effect. I've been walking, reading, talking with Elaine, as we contemplate what we want to do with our lives. It almost feels as if the impending baby is motivating me more strongly than anything in the past to establish some goals, to create more forcefully an identity with the world. Yet I'm simultaneously serene, more established and settled and centered than I can recall.

Seeing creatures at the coast is one of the finer pleasures of the trip for me. The first evening a fleet of dolphins played, leaping in arcs, flashing their tails, circling and undulating along, some so close to shore that their bottlenosed faces were clearly visible. They sported among themselves for the last hour of the day, disappearing as the sun sank below the far meeting of water and sky.

Shell hunting on the point of the cape gave me more graceful and unbroken shells of perfection than I could possibly carry home. Pelicans glided over the surface of the gulf and soared above in formation — wide strong wings and long tough beaks. At the tip of the point they roosted. It seemed like thousands, although probably only a few hundred. Debating how close to go, we opted to leave them their place and their peace.

I was surprised to find fearless raccoons by the salt water. Two critters broke into our garbage can last night, staring balefully into our flashlight beam, poised, waiting for us to go away. We did. They left the corn cobs on the deck when they were done.

A solitary walk past the dunes of the state park this morning left me wondering, as Pony shuffled around inside and I rested, how hard will it be to come by such time alone? When I get it, will I be preoccupied with thoughts of my child? Children? What joys might they bring me — discoveries, wonders, perceptions, currently beyond my ken? What pains? What agonies of worry might I suffer over them? When I'm afraid to let them go, will I remember my fears of being trapped?

I can't stay in my second trimester forever, but right now it seems like a fine place to be. Pony's presence makes the pregnancy and the future a reality but I'm not so big as to be uncomfortable, and Pony's not out in the world yet, overwhelming me with change and newness.

May 18

An odd and disturbing dream this morning. Rick was with me but I was home in Short Hills with my family. Mom and Pop and Rob and Pete were there, although the dream concentrated mostly on Mom. Basically, the house was falling in (literally). In several rooms of our large home (grown huge in the dream), sheets of rain and water were pouring through the ceilings. The plaster was bulging. I desperately urged my mother to do something about it immediately, to let me do something, or to evacuate. She was blandly unaffected, merely saying we didn't need those rooms anyway and she'd just close them off. We then went to the third floor of the house where the same thing was happening. Suddenly the roof over an entire room gave way completely, then part of the floor near us, toppling a roll-away bed to the floor below. I raced downstairs horrified that, although my mother had just stepped out of the room that had collapsed, she still seemed unruffled by the danger.

Downstairs, we were all at the dining room table getting ready to have dinner. The maid, who seemed a bit tearful and neurotic, had prepared and would serve the food. I concentrated on my father now (who was, in fact, sitting in my mother's seat), trying to explain the danger of the collapse above. The whole house would soon give way. With terror, I saw that the ceiling in the next room was now slowly leaking water. No one seemed to understand.

Suddenly I saw a car driving in our back yard, heading toward the house. Before I had a chance to puzzle too long, it crashed through the picture window and into the living room! We soon realized this wasn't simply an accident, but some maniac bent on destruction. He began purposefully driving through walls. It quickly became obvious, as we scattered about, that he was specifically after me. I ducked and dodged and finally escaped out the kitchen door. As I fled through the yard, I worried about the others, but realized I could only protect myself. As I woke up it seemed I had eluded him.

While this is the most disturbing dream I've had in a while, it's not the first I've had where I'm reimmersed, as an adult, in my nuclear family (fully intact with my father still alive). Usually Rick is not in the dream.

Elaine suggested an interpretation of this morning's wanderings that struck me with startling accuracy yet I had not even considered, or been consciously aware of, such an underlying dilemma. The dream may reflect a conflict I feel about the destruction (or displacement) of my birth family by my becoming a mother, relinquishing my role as daughter to take over the role of mother. Marriage didn't seem to have any such effect but that could well be because I don't subscribe to any stereotypical notions of being a wife. I am comfortable maintaining my own, known, identity while being married to Rick (although I do recall some premarital jitters that somehow this would not be the case). But *motherhood*. It's so unknown. There's no trial period. You can't quite live with the baby first to see if it will work out and to discover if you're compatible! You're quite stuck with it unless you have to face the horror and guilt of losing a baby to death. Guilt only because you recognized an ambivalence and worked with it, realizing and examining the future changes with an excitement tinged with fear.

May 23

Home feels good. I'm invigorated from the week with Elaine. I feel goal-directed and centered. We've got parallels: I'm going to make time to write, she's going to procure a teaching job. Ultimately, I want to move the world as a writer. Ultimately, she wants to move the world as a judge.

The guideline for our week of mental calisthenics was Barbara Sher's *Wishcraft*. I hate the title but the guts are good. There was one section where Sher was talking about fears and balancing and guilt. One gentleman was quoted as saying how much happier he would have been if his mother had been less single-minded with concern for him and the household and had instead come into his room bursting with excitement about some poem she had written. That strikes a chord. When parents are too self-sacrificing, I think the children sense it and just feel guilty. Adults frequently feel responsible for their parents' happiness or unhappiness. It seems inevitable that if the parent had nothing else of importance to focus on but the child, the child will grow up feeling responsible for parental equilibrium. So the key is balancing, an elusive goal that nearly always needs readjustment.

I felt irritated and hurt yesterday while talking to Mom. She sounded depressed and I felt like it was my fault she was depressed. I know that's ridiculous. But what upset me more was discussion of her travel plans. At least every few years she goes somewhere exotic. This year she's debating between Papua, New Guinea and Turkey. I asked for her thinking on the matter. She's wanted to go to New Guinea for many years but just hasn't done it yet. This particular trip is more than twice what she usually spends, she says.

She doesn't know if there's even any space left. Yes, she's planning to call this week. The trip is in July. The Turkey trip is interesting, too, she says. It departs September 23.

I'm astounded. Bereft. This is when my baby's due! I felt all this despite the fact that I've already told her I think Rick and I want the first week or two on our own. I guess I still wanted her around, for questions on the phone, and to come down anyway, early, if I changed my mind. And anger, I feel that too. Her *only* daughter giving birth to her *first* child and Mom's first grandchild to boot. Almost total disbelief on my part. Don't you care? Other relatives and friends, especially Rick's family, just assume she's bursting with excitement and dying to be involved, informed, supportive. And here she is going off to Turkey (well, considering going off to Turkey) when I'm about to birth my first child.

I can still step back a little, and I'm trying to do so more. I feel critical of her when I think she's not leading her own life, when she lets life just pass her by. So now when she's clearly taking charge of her own life, doing what *she* wants, I feel rejected.

What if the situation were reversed? My daughter is grown, her baby is due, and there's a trip I'd really like to take. My daughter has already told me she doesn't want me on her doorstep the day after birth. She wants a few weeks. What do I do? Society might call me selfish if I went ahead with my plans but I would prefer to call myself independent. How do I know what I'll feel about this future pregnant daughter? Is that the heart of it? How does my mother feel about me? Does she love me? Does she love my baby? Does she even believe my baby will exist?

May 24

I'm miffed. The prenatal exercise classes at the Y will be ending for the summer due to lack of interest. I've had only two other classmates for two months now. They're pleasant but I miss the networking effect and support group feel of having a few more. I was bummed out to hear this news, as now part of my carefully crafted social structure begins to crumble. Isolation hangs heavy on anyone's hands. I may fare better than many, as I often seek solitude. And my work is solitary. Yet perhaps because of that, I feel a strong need to establish a group of friends or at least contacts. Of course, my fear is that after the baby is born all opportunity will be lost. I will be struggling to regain survival equilibrium. Battling fatigue. Turning simple acts like laundry and grocery shopping into strategic events.

An article in *Hippocrates*, a health magazine, talks of pregnancy dreams and how denying their significance or refusing to acknowledge the anxieties inherent in such a significant life transition can cause more difficult labor. It's hard to relax completely, they say, when, in the back of your mind, you're simultaneously denying yet worrying about some of the less-than-rosy aspects of motherhood. If that's the case, and the converse is true, I should be a limp noodle during labor! I mull over and analyze to death my ambivalence.

Another article discussed the variety of prenatal tests available and their impact on creating or fostering the tentative pregnancy. While acknowledging *all* pregnancy is something of a state of limbo, the tentative pregnancy refers to the possibility of voluntarily terminating the pregnancy. Not the baby, of course, the pregnancy. Defective future babies are removed from their life support systems.

Why such a conflict for me? I'm still pro-choice. Clearly. A woman's body is her own. And if the potential seed of life, no matter how baby-like in appearance, *needs her* and to be inside her to survive, she—the existing individual—has the proper power and authority (moral and otherwise) to decide. So why do I ramble? Where does my confusion come from? From feeling Pony move. From looking at enough books to know what Pony looks like. Pony, at 23 weeks and into the 24th, is a little baby. I believe that every time I feel a roll or a turn, a kick or a punch. Even though I can still ignore Pony and let this little one slip from my consciousness as I concentrate on other activities, I view this baby in a way I never before understood pregnancy. Pregnancies were legally terminable states of being in women up to 28 weeks. That is the legal definition of fetus viability. The earlier done, the safer. But allowed up to more than halfway through gestation. Morally acceptable, according to the law.

Why didn't I know this before? I was never so cavalier as to classify abortion as birth control. I knew it was serious. I never wanted to face one. Yet I knew having that control over my life, *my* life, was crucial. Crucial to all women. Perhaps it is primarily the pull of reality and this baby. This wanted baby who is still so much a potential. Who, in the mysteries of life and death, may in fact still not make it out into the world alive. Stories of premature deliveries flutter constantly in the periphery of my mind. Is the confusion from the devastating imbalance of having the power to end life but not having the same definitive power to maintain it?

May 25

This morning, I'm exhausted. I was exhausted at the end of yesterday — the second very busy, intense day in a row. Yet restful sleep eluded me last night. I dozed off almost immediately but seemed to half-wake throughout the night. I know I was up to use the bathroom at 2:30 a.m., and it felt more like 4:30 a.m.! And by 7 o'clock I was aware of continual low grade discomfort in my lower back and on the lower sides. I'm surprised and can't figure it out. I'm optimistic this is only a temporary aberration but fog in with a small sense of defeat at the thought that such things may plague the rest of the pregnancy. And knowing this level of fatigue may only be a shadow of what's to come this fall doesn't help. Exhaustion is hard to write about. My mind blanks, my pen suspends itself above the paper, my eyes glaze over, and I'm not even aware any of these things are occurring.

My dream last night was noteworthy mainly because it was so clear. I was with a large crowd of people at some high-rise building by the ocean. A hurricane was supposed to be coming. People were a little worried but, besides clouds, the only noticeable change was the tide being sucked very far out. Then it began to rush in. The waves lapped up as far as the building. Everyone else was sure that would be it, that would be the extent of the storm. I felt differently. As I was heading toward a door to go up a flight or two, waves crashed through the first-level glass doors. People began running.

As I climbed, the tide receded, and most people waited on the beach to get in boats. I felt that was a mistake and was proved right when water flooded the second floor. I moved from my third floor room (it was sort of like a dorm) up a few more floors. Others were with me but most were still trying to get in boats. I felt safe there and woke up.

June 1

Summer has swarmed and swamped us with 95-degree heat and 90 percent humidity. It isn't pleasant but being pregnant, at least at this stage, has not made it worse. My problem is the lower right side of my back. I don't understand why it keeps acting up when I lie down, attempting to sleep in all the approved and previously comfortable positions. My books indicate it is simply one of the uterosacral ligaments; two of those attach to the uterus from the rear and another set of round ligaments anchor it in the front in the groin. The midwives mentioned possible pain from the frontal ligaments, and discussed backache in general, but not this pain specifically. It's been going on a week and a half now. After a week of lousy sleep, I started using the heating pad (which only helped a little) and ultimately Tylenol (which gives me about three or four hours of relief). I can usually fall asleep and then awaken around 4:00 a.m. (sometimes 2:00 a.m.), prodded awake by the discomfort, unable to return to sleep. So, for four nights now I've taken Tylenol. The pain is generally better during the day athough sometimes while sitting, as now, it makes its presence felt. Sometimes I'm horrified at the thought it might last and only grow worse with the pregnancy. And other times I think *June*, we're to June, into the summer heat, the last leg. From the wintery start in January, I've always thought of the last leg in the long hot stretch of summer.

Swimming, walking (especially on the beaches), and prenatal classes are keeping me moving. I couldn't believe it yesterday. Getting on the scale after four days away, I tipped it beyond the next major notch. Total gain is 13 pounds which is right on the chart for 24 weeks, but I have been feeling very large. I seem to be falling into the same myopic vision I've seen with so many other pregnant women. I don't feel like I look pregnant, I feel like I look fat. My self-image is so much better when I'm wearing maternity clothes that scream "Mommy" in their cut and design than when I wear others that simply seem to make room.

I haven't been noticing my dreams much recently, and I think it's due to my interrupted sleep patterns. I wonder if I'm even reaching the REM state? Yet I must be sleeping better than I think I am because, for the last week at least, I've been functioning well above fatigue levels.

One thing I've avoided for months now is addressing the second miscarriage. The opportunity was at hand this past weekend. May 26th. The start of Memorial Day weekend. Our third anniversary. A year to the day of the second miscarriage. The day itself this year was hectic. Not at all conducive to reflection or even romance. It was full of preparation for the extended combination of celebration and work (for Rick) on Kiawah Island, South Carolina. He had a conference on employment law Friday and Saturday but the surrounding time, through Monday, was ours.

Hectic is an understatement. By nightfall Thursday, it felt like hell. We'd both been running a mile a minute finishing up necessary chores before departure. We left two and a half hours later than our already amended departure time of 2:00 p.m. The drive, with a dinner stop, was seven hours. My back was pinching progressively. And worst, I had been mentally predisposed to a rewarding, loving, nurturing anniversary. I think to make up for last year. Last year that is such a blur — so obliterated from my memory. Last year when I miscarried. *Again.*

On May 25th a year ago, we also went to the beach. Wrightsville Beach, for the day. It was Sunday or Monday. Three hours away. A long drive, but we left early enough and it was worth it. Sun and sand encrusted, we had seafood at a local place for dinner. We drove home through the dusk and descending night. We talked of Rick's current job and possible change. The new firm looked like it would meet his needs so much better. He was so upset over leaving the firm that had hired him out of Charleston after only eight months with them, yet he was equally unhappy there. The new firm had talked with him three or four times already, and things looked very encouraging.

I recall feeling a little out of it physically, that day, feeling unattractive in my bathing suit. Only nine weeks pregnant yet bloated. As we walked the beach that day, we (as usual) kept noticing all the other obviously pregnant women and the little babies. May 25th was a good day. Or was it May 24th? It doesn't matter, I know, but I can't grasp the rest of the sequence except knowing *it* happened the night of the 26th.

Perhaps the beach was on the 24th, because the next morning I started spotting. Very lightly. We had made love the night before. (Doctors had reassured us many times after the first miscarriage that intercourse does not cause miscarriages.) It may precipitate the timing of one, but our first ultrasound showed a specific set of facts: development long ended.

Back to the chronology of this loss. I called the doctor's office that morning and went in. I was angry because I hadn't even had my first prenatal appointment yet. When I had called to make one after the positive home pregnancy test, they set it up for four or five weeks later—"the earliest opening available." So I hadn't even seen a midwife or doctor yet. But spotting? Yes, they'd see me right away. I was seen by Dr. Paul Harden. And I'm astonished that I had to look up the practice in the Yellow Pages today to remember his name. Of the two midwives there and the three doctors I had been in contact with, he was my favorite. There was something indefinable, perhaps, in his gentle manner and honest approach that made me very comfortable with him. He seemed to take a personal interest in my care. The next series of appointments were all with him. We did some tests later, looking for a cause. I felt I was his patient, not a patient of the entire practice. Yet I had to find his name in the phone book.

I denied and denied and denied. I numbed myself. I went into slow motion. I prevented myself from perceiving as much as possible.

I went to the doctor's office May 25th or 26th and was seen by Dr. Harden. My cervix was closed but I was spotting. (Yes, I know Doctor.) The spotting is light and can be very common in pregnancy. (Yes, I know Doctor.) But I think we should get you an ultrasound to see what's going on. (Yes, I agree Doctor.)

So I drank and drank but don't remember drinking. I don't remember if I went to work at all that day, nor do I remember calling to say I couldn't come in. I was back at the same radiology office, sitting in the same waiting room, with the same full bladder. Nine weeks pregnant and spotting. If I lost it this time, I thought mildly, there's really a problem. No emotion. Just a repeat, a bland repeat, of the thoughts I'd had after the first miscarriage. Once is OK. Not OK, of course, but allowed. They're common. It doesn't mean anything about the future. The same older people in the waiting room. A few children. Why were they all there? Mammograms for the women? Cancer treatments for the obviously sick and elderly? X-rays for the young ones? I didn't know. I could only leaf through the magazines. *People*. A promotional guide to the industry and businesses of Raleigh. I think I read an article about the cast of "L.A. Law." My bladder ached. And I waited.

To the receptionist. Sat down. Again. Insurance card out. Yes, I'd been there before. Next, waiting in an internal sanctum. Not so long this time. Into the gown. Onto the table. Rick wasn't with me. He didn't go to the doctor's with me that morning either. Work, I suppose. I don't remember. I wasn't upset with him. He couldn't be there. Perhaps I wished I couldn't be there either.

The ultrasound seemed to go a little more quickly this time. Again, the operator told me nothing. Just to go back to my doctor's office, and he'd explain what they saw. I don't recall if any seeds of hope had been scattered. I don't recall. As I was leaving, she dashed and crushed any stray seedlings with an off hand remark. I understood her to mean, "Better luck next time," but I think in fact it was something like, "See you next time," or "Maybe next time." I didn't have time to mull it long. Truth was only two minutes down the road. Around the two blocks into the doctors' peach, mint, and grey waiting room. Very tasteful.

I was ushered back into Dr. Harden's office. He seemed genuinely unhappy, in a most professional manner, to have to give me the results. Despite the tipped uterus, he said, there was no ambiguity. The ultrasound showed five weeks of fetal growth. Period. Not nine. It may have been any empty sac. I don't recall if that was said or not. There was no heartbeat, no doubt, no baby. He recommended a D&C. For a missed miscarriage. No, he didn't mind waiting a while if that's what I preferred, to see if I'd abort on my own. I preferred. There was no hope this time. Not really. And then I don't remember. I don't remember going to work. I don't remember going home. I don't remember calling Rick.

It was either that evening (again after dinner around 7:30) or the next evening, whichever was our anniversary. Number two on number two. How symmetrical. How poetic.

I don't remember the bleeding or the clots. I don't remember how late I stayed up. Was it such an instant replay? "Is it live or is it Memorex?" I do remember the pain. Again around 2:00 or 2:30 a.m., lasting about half an hour. It felt worse than the first time. Yet the ultimate tissue passed was so much smaller. Loose, not formed into any recognizable placenta.

The next day and the following days are all lost, but one memory stands out. The next morning at the doctor's office. I went to be looked over and to have them look at the collected tissue. Was my cervix still dilated? Was the abortion complete? The cervix was nearly closed. The abortion looked complete. No one asked me if I wanted the tissue this time. I was told (again) if the bleeding increased or I felt any pain or my temperature rose (I should be taking it at regular intervals), I was to call them immediately. I knew all that. Possibility of infection.

And then I got my RhoGAM shot to insure future pregnancies, even though I probably didn't need it. A blood system was unlikely to have developed. I cried as I left the office and sat in my car. Tears I can't conjure up anymore. Not deep sobs but rivulets of tears. Rick was not with me.

The following week is barren. I don't recall how those at work found out. Evelyn gave me a book, *Ended Beginnings*, with a note but I think that was a little later. Both meant a lot to me. She had miscarried a baby at five months, I think, a number of years ago. They later adopted their daughter and are beginning to plan for the adoption of their second child. Medically, emotionally, I don't know what happened.

I stayed home a few days, I think, then tried to return to work. It was painfully obvious I wasn't ready. As dry-eyed as I'd been at home, whenever anyone would sympathetically ask how I was doing or express sorrow, I would start to cry. Tears that frightened me. I could not control them. I couldn't stop. My friends and co-workers wisely sent me home. Their support was strong. Practically, I was hardly in any shape to handle any crisis calls that day or next week. They covered my Monday shift for me. Was I out another week? I had comp time and I used it along with my sick leave. What did I do at home? I don't know. It feels like amnesia. When I went back to work the next time I was better. I didn't cry. I did my job.

I have one more memory in the void until July. At the end of the first week in June, Rick's potential new employer wanted to take the two of us out to dinner. Two younger partners, their wives, and us, at the Hope Valley Country Club. To see if we drooled or ate with our fingers, we joked. But basically we knew it was one final step before an offer, and a pleasant one. Their insurance, an attempt to confirm a good match, that everyone would be happy with the arrangement.

I was a little nervous, which was odd. Things like that don't get me nervous. I think it was because I didn't know who to be or how to be. The real Ellen was numb and grieving over a miscarriage. Two miscarriages. That's what I would have been willing to talk about, what I *wanted* to talk about, to explain my subdued and inattentive state. I didn't think it would come up, and it didn't. The dinner was quiet, uneventful, and a bit awkward. No one knew what to talk about. So Rick and I perceived it, anyway. But he got the job and hasn't regretted the move. In fact, he started within days of the offer. This was an unanticipated upheaval. His offer to stay on with the old firm for up to two months, if they needed it, was summarily rejected. They suggested an immediate departure. *C'est la vie.* The new guys were glad to have him. At the time, it was occasionally awkward, as he was now only a few floors up in the same building. But by the end of July, the new firm had completed its long-laid plans, packed their bags and relocated to a new highrise.

What else, beyond these job gyrations, helped preoccupy me? What else steered my vision away from anything internal? In June, we also began looking for another house. Never mind that we already owned the one in Raleigh and had only owned it since September. If Rick was going to be working on the far side of Durham, he was looking at a 45-minute commute. For professional reasons, I was restless in my job. I was no longer pregnant but the tests were all encouraging. There should be no reason we wouldn't have as many babies as we wanted. We hadn't established ties in the neighborhood. Why not move now, if we could? Resettle. Start over. New job, maybe new pregnancy. Why settle in deeper in a community we planned to abandon? More likely, why not substitute one upheaval (one at least we could control and manage to some extent) for another? One that had hit us broadside. One that we could do little about.

So, in June we looked at houses. In early July, I went to the beach. The isolated and windswept Outer Banks. With Elaine for the week; Rick joining us for the last half. My favorite beach. It did little for me. I felt nothing. Beautiful isolated beaches have always either calmed me or exhilarated me. Not this time. The house was ugly and the weather, hot. The only inkling I had of what was going on came one evening. We were alone, early in the week and, with only brief light tears, I told Elaine I thought maybe I was still grieving the second miscarriage. But I don't recollect that I had a lot to say about it. My journal was with me, and it is devoid of relevant entries. No more insight or direct consideration of the lost baby for another week or so.

Back at work after that July vacation, I met with the shelter director to discuss some problems that had occurred in her absence the prior month. As her supervisor, I had taken over the in-charge role at the shelter. However, because of her overall competence, I had been able to leave the vast bulk of the operation entirely up to her in the previous months. Thus, I was unaware of the day-to-day mechanics at the shelter and unaware of how her staff resented my acting as leader and not consulting them on certain actions and conversations. They preferred operation on a consensus basis. I tend to operate more hierarchically.

Their displeasure came back to me through this meeting with Tanyer in mid-July. A professional analysis or reaction was completely absent on my part. I found myself enraged at them, and then bursting into miserable tears. I was mortified and horrified. I had just come back from a relaxing week at the beach! What was going on inside me? I was astute enough to figure out that this overblown reaction signalled a certain level of derangement—a clear cry for support, guidance, and help that I wasn't getting.

Where had I gotten the phone numbers? One of my visits to the doctors' office for the testing of my systems. On their bulletin boards there was one sheet of paper (in a corner) labeled "Grieving" listing three groups or organizations with brief descriptions. For whatever reason (description? location? someone who answered the phone?) I got in touch with Parent Care. Meeting the first and third Thursday of each month in a spare room at some church at 7:30 in the evening. For parents who had lost children under one year. Yes, miscarriages were definitely included. Rick and I made plans to go.

June 4

How can this be? The past miscarriages, Parent Care, my pregnancy, and my future baby seem to be receding into the background of my life. My excitement and attentions focus on my other writing projects and on the fledgling formation of a new professional theater group in the area. I fell into Karyn and Lena's theater plans by accident (however serendipitous), but I'm infused with energy. Working on my own first play (tentatively titled *Traveling Light*) and increasing my exposure to theater (reading more plays, seeing more plays) throws my vision simultaneously far into the future and deeply into the present. Neither place seems to include the demands of a small child. I feel so thrilled and focused with my own life, what *I* can do, myself, not how I can grow by helping a small needy one I have had a hand in creating.

Swimming this morning, my first time on a Saturday, invigorated me. The water was very cold, however, as the outside temperatures dropped from 90 degrees earlier this week to 60 degrees at noon today! But an astonishingly gorgeous day—blue, blue sky with the occasional white puff of cloud. The hypnotic movement and breathing in the water cleanse my body and clear my head. Not clear it, exactly, loosen it up to further thought. Today I mulled, lap after lap, the characters of *Traveling Light* and the structure that would immerse them.

It's funny. The play has been without a working title since I conceived it last year. But last night, my dreams focused on this project. Less a dream than active intellectual thinking while asleep! This title came to me then.

When am I going to finish the nursery? So far we've bought a crib and a diaper bag. There's so much still to do! I need to find a rug; order a dresser/changing table; install some shelves near the changing table; get a car seat; order the Baby Matey body carrier; consider our need for a stroller; get a playpen, a highchair, a baby monitor to hear the kid from elsewhere in the house, and a swing; procure a cradle or bedside basket for the first few months of night life by our bedside; get a mobile for the crib and bright pictures for the walls; get sheets and bumper pads, a baby bath, and all the baby clothes. . . . Is it endless? Do I make it endless?

June 6

In the late afternoon and early evening light of Saturday, Rick and I planted two trees. Peter sent them for my birthday, five weeks ago, but they only arrived this week. A dwarf Moonglow Pear and a dwarf Seckle Pear. Rick dug the hard red clay soil. I mixed the fertilizer and stirred in the peat. He held each tree as I put good potting soil at the bottom, heavily watered with Miracle Grow, and added the clay and peat mixture. As the holes filled, we covered them to the top and patted them down together. I topped them off with a layer of peat and let the garden hose trickle by each tree for half an hour.

Each tree looks pathetic, dead. A three-foot barren stalk pruned to the skinny trunk for proper transplant. Will they live? Grow? Thrive, even? One season? A year? Three years? Will we feel they've made it at any one point? I feel as if one tree's for Pony and one's for us—our marriage, our life in this house. It's dangerous to so label them this early. I'll be so sad if they die.

Two other things happened this weekend. A package of layette items arrived from cousins John and Mary. It was sweet of them and so needed! It's the first baby gift we've received. And last night I talked endlessly with Alice D. (the wife of a partner in Rick's firm). It was only the second time we met, yet we talked as if we'd known each other for years. Like floodgates opening. We talked about hope and fear, miscarriages and infertility.

She had been trying to get pregnant for years when she discovered her tubes are blocked. She's been participating in the in vitro fertilization program at Duke. So far, she has succeeded in becoming pregnant once. Five embryos were implanted (or identified), and she made it to seven weeks before she began to bleed. She had three days of bloody limbo before her progesterone finally sank low enough for the doctors to tell her that this time was all over. She, too, didn't know what to look for through the blood.

"If you pass tissue," the doctor says, "it's all over." What would tissue look like? "Like meat," she was told. That didn't help her. It wouldn't have helped me. We compared notes graphically. "Was that it?" she wanted to know. I said it sounded like it to me. What she described sounded more like my second nine-week miscarriage with minimal development as opposed to the tough corded placenta I passed the first time.

I told her of my hysteria in October. A strong description of my reaction, but I was tense, tearful, upset. My period was a few days late. Another day and I was ready to buy a pregnancy test. We had been trying. It had been four months. Plausible. Conceivable. Perhaps conceived. But my period came, heavy and crampy. Near the end, I passed a clot that looked like tissue. It was spongy in texture, bigger than a nickel, smaller than a quarter, and tan. I clutched. I put it in a cup. I called my doctors in Raleigh. I was clearly upset, and I imagine Dr. Harden was trying to calm me down, but he just made me angrier. I wanted the tissue sent to pathology to find out if, in fact, I'd had a third miscarriage. I wanted to know. If I had, there were several other tests to do on me and on Rick. There would be a myriad of issues to face. A third miscarriage would create a significant history of spontaneous abortion. It would verify that we had a problem.

Harden advised against a pathology test. Either he didn't think I miscarried or he thought that, if I had, it didn't matter since it was so early in my cycle. He finally said, in a voice that sounded simply fed up, "If you're so upset about it, bring it in." Hardly a ringing endorsement of support.

There was another reason I was so fearful. A year before I met Rick I was involved with another man. I was being fairly careful with birth control but was not on the pill. My actions that month had definitely left some room for error. My period was late. I was never sure exactly how late because I didn't keep records of each appearance, and trivia like that does not stay in my mind. I performed a pregnancy test with a negative result, and the next day my period came. I think it was about two weeks late. I bled heavily and was a little crampy, and I passed an unusual looking clot. Knowing almost nothing in detail about pregnancy and abortions, I noticed this clot and wondered if, in fact, I had miscarried. All I felt was relief. If I had been pregnant, I now wouldn't have to face an elective abortion. If I had been pregnant (I felt at the time) I had almost willed it away.

The clot I passed then, clear in my mind, was the same type I passed this October. If I had miscarried now, I had miscarried then. I would have had four miscarriages. The problem would be mine.

Instead of going to Raleigh, where they had just made me feel like an hysterical idiot, I looked in the Yellow Pages. We'd only lived in Durham three weeks but I needed to find a local OB-GYN practice anyway. I found a practice in Durham that used midwives (the Women's Clinic) and a private MD practice with midwives in Chapel Hill. That's how I hooked up with my care providers. Only later did I confirm their good reputation in the field.

I explained my situation to the receptionist, and she told me to come in that afternoon. They were supportive and did send the sample to pathology. The physical exam showed that my cervix was closed. Maybe I had calmed down; it was now seven hours after I had discovered the clot. Or maybe their attitude was better.

The lab report was inconclusive, perhaps as Harden suspected it would be. They could not confirm whether or not I had passed "products of conceptus." So I never did know. I probably never will. I actively chose to believe those two incidents were not miscarriages. But all of me, every fiber, doesn't feel so sure.

And now we're supposed to pick a pediatrician within three weeks. Because if Pony were born, Pony might live.

June 7

Flight from Chicago to Portland, Oregon. This morning I had a major scare. Rick had been asking me if I had felt Pony that morning or last night. Suddenly it seemed as if I hadn't felt Pony much at all recently! I mean I had, but the movements seemed so much weaker I'd barely been noticing them. Had I just been too busy? Was Pony taking a rest? Shifted to a more comfortable position? Or was something wrong—was Pony growing weaker day by day from some yet undiagnosed condition? To die. To die while I'm in Canada with Nancy.

Since my scary hour this morning when Pony refused to cooperate and move, I've relaxed. She or he is kicking now and again, some movements as strong as ever. I think I'm simply more used to the movements, so I don't notice them as much. And I have been focusing my attention outward, not inward. When I do focus inside, quietly sitting and waiting, Pony is easier to perceive.

June 8

I'll be with Nancy for a week. Two days in Portland before we wend our way toward Vancouver Island, British Columbia.

Today, I think I was conned. Does it matter? Do I care? I do care and I'm not sure why, given the circumstances. I was browsing an hour and a half in Powell's Book Store and made a totally luxurious purchase. Two, in fact: May Sarton's *After the Stroke*, her latest journal, reporting her struggle to health; and an overview book on theater management to provide further guidance for Eccentric Circles, Karyn and Lena's new theater company. Somehow these purchases capped off and personified earlier events, crystallizing my life. I was feeling lucky, privileged, happy, fortunate, blessed . . . how many adjectives can I find?

As we left Powell's, a skinny unkempt woman approached us. She was in her late 30s with brown hair below her shoulders. Her white blazer needed cleaning yet it appeared that she had pulled herself together as much as possible. She was near tears. She asked for information. Did we know of any churches with an outreach or benevolent program? She had no place to stay tonight. It was 5:30. She was to start a new job tomorrow but would receive no paycheck for two weeks. She had tried churches and shelters (mentioning a few) and struck out. She was not battered. She didn't have children. She fell through the cracks, she said.

All this is plausible. Nancy suggested Baloney Joe's. I thought this was a restaurant and that she was suggesting the woman try there for information. Later, in the car, I learned it was a shelter that doesn't usually turn people away. The woman told us they weren't helpful.

The woman said she had located a place to stay (only $40 per month) but all she had to her name was $15 plus 50 cents for phone calls. She said early on that she wasn't asking for money. She was fairly insistent on that point. She just wanted suggestions of where to get help—a church or something.

I felt helpless, not knowing the area resources. Nancy couldn't come up with much.

The woman seemed proud yet distraught. Trying hard to hold together, not to beg. I offered to write the woman a check to the landlord who could rent her the room she mentioned and told her she could mail me the money later if she was able. She was grateful but feared the check wouldn't be acceptable to the landlord; others had cash and the room would go to one of them. So I decided to give her $20 cash and my name and address should she be able to pay me back, but I was not counting on seeing the money again. She asked if I thought a postal money order would be the best way to return it. I said that would be fine.

She seemed so genuine, so at a loss, so relieved and surprised and grateful for the money. So what's the problem? I did a good deed.

One block farther down the street a man, nicely dressed in a casual fashion and sitting in a red sports car, called to us as we passed. He asked us if we had believed that woman and said he had seen us give her something. He explained that he was an actor and had been watching her technique. She works this block. Three weeks ago, she approached him and a friend and the friend gave her money. He told the friend the same thing: she was a con approaching people regularly with hard luck stories.

I was dismayed and angry, betrayed. At him. At her. At me. Was it true? Did it matter? She wasn't drunk or on drugs when she spoke to us, but that could have been the reason for seeking money. Whatever her needs, she clearly could use the money more than I. What must her life be like to do this, even if it was a straight con? That's what I hang onto now. It was still a good deed. Yet, what? I never respond to street requests for money. I say a brusque or quick or quiet "sorry" and move on. I give to organized charities; it's more effective than giving to individuals on the streets. But I've learned that this long-held belief isn't necessarily true. I know how organized charities can fail the individual. She touched me. I believed her. And it hurts to think it was all skilled, conscious, and manipulative. That someone would do that. And anger at myself that my senses failed me, that I was wrong in my assessment of her.

June 10

It's 9:30 p.m. and the sky is still light with sunset. I look past large pines and, if I crane my neck, I can see the harbor. A stunning day. I'm procrastinating before I bathe for the evening. I'm not fond of evening baths for cleaning purposes; they're nice for relaxation but I prefer a nice morning shower to get clean. But in this small Bed & Breakfast outside Victoria that's not possible.

It's been a long day, and I only had an hour's nap, but the late setting sun has me fooled. I've been feeling sort of swollen recently, and a poor mattress or lack of sleep makes it worse. Last night in Port Angeles created both problems. The heat was up too high and my metabolism is already cranked up, so I sweltered.

The ferry ride over to Victoria was pleasant, and we left the wet gloom over the United States and found Vancouver Island under cloud-dotted blue skies.

An afternoon walk on my own yielded two discoveries. A charming male colt, just beyond the scrawniness of birth but still on unsteady stick legs, graced one field and farther along the country road, in another field, three small children frolicked with butterfly nets. They ran 'round and 'round after butterflies and each other, calling out happy hellos to the passing stranger.

Despite the setting, I'm frustrated and sad. Nancy and I are not communicating well. I can't place my finger on the dynamics. Have our interests diverged? Am I just not up for a trip of hopping about rather than settling into a serene place for communing with nature and each other? We've known each other more than 15 years but it's been a long time since we've traveled together.

June 17

A week without writing. Where to start? As the week progressed with Nancy, things got both better and worse. Pony seemed more vibrant but I may have been getting more tired. Nancy and I crabbed at each other now and then, getting impatient with our differences. Such differences seem so silly yet they accumulated space between us. For example, many times as we'd drive about looking for a parking space on the crowded streets, there might appear an empty spot on the opposite side of the street. I would call it to Nancy's attention (with enthusiasm in direct proportion to the length of time we'd been circling the area) expecting, then suggesting, a U-turn to claim the spot. Invariably, Nancy would avoid such decisive action and drive around the block, only to have the space predictably filled by the time we returned. I imagine she perceived me as impatient and aggressive while I perceived her as meek and unassertive. This was disconcerting. When we had a few days together last December, it was as if time had wrought no changes despite our lack of time together in the last 10 years.

For the first five years after college, even though she was in Edinburgh, Scotland, we continued to be intimate friends although primarily through the mail. Over the next five years, as we each moved into the work world, lengthening silences cropped up between our calls or letters. But we always felt that our friendship was firmly established, rooted for life, and neither time apart nor gaps in communication would harm it. Visits were few and brief during this period. So now, when we claim a week of time, what happened? I'm not sure. The trip was hardly a total bust. We did talk and found an old common ground of silly humor, but it didn't feel the same. There are lots of possible reasons: we didn't give ourselves adjustment time to live and travel together after so much time apart; we set expectations too high; I was tired, less up for traveling than I thought; or—a sad thought—we may have changed and grown apart. It *felt* that way which was why I found it upsetting. I'd hate to grieve for such a special friendship spanning so much time. Have I changed so much?

One of the ridiculously fun things we did on our return pass through Port Angeles was visit the Psychic Fair. On the drive up to the ferry from Portland we had commented how neither of us had ever gone to a palm reader or psychic, and we were both curious. We vowed we'd have to do that some time. Lo and behold, a handdrawn poster in one of the restaurants we checked out for dinner advertised this fair in an upstairs banquet room on the day we would return. We certainly had to go.

Sunday was blue and bright and clear. We had decided to pick our psychic(s) on our own intuition rather than deciding beforehand what service (palms, tea leaves, tarot) to choose. There were only six tables, one being a bookstore display. Several of the all-purpose psychics had brochures, including ours, Elva May. Subsequently, we learned that Elva May may have been the best choice. She had trained several of the others there. Most of the seers and visitors were older women but what the heck. Elva May was the most down-to-earth in appearance.

Nancy and I each paid $15 for 15 minutes. Because it wasn't

crowded or perhaps because she liked us, we each spent over half an hour with her. No dark booths, flowing robes, or crystal balls; each psychic sat at her rectangular folding table on the perimeter of the room. I went first.

Elva May looked younger than her 54 years and eight grandchildren. She was quite willing to share information about herself. She was pleased to learn I was a Taurus and Rick a Leo—a combination not guaranteed to work according to the stars, she said, but she and her husband are also a Taurus and a Leo and have been happily married for 32 years. That seemed like such a long time, I was shocked. No, she didn't divine our astrological pairing. She asked our birthdays. In fact, Elva May asked a lot of questions. Some open-ended, some specific. When I balked a bit and gave vague answers, explaining I was a skeptic, she assured me that was better. Too many gratuitous facts blurred her readings.

I was disappointed she used a tarot deck as her tool. I've used the tarot too much myself, along with the I Ching, as meditation and exploration tools. She also said too many things that were too general and too far off the truth, insofar as describing the present situation. The things that were close to home appeared to be good educated guesses. Despite all this, I really liked her.

Elva May says, with certainty, that Pony is a girl (although she speculated briefly about twins, discarding the thought with an appraising glance and a "No, you're not big enough"). I had asked her to discuss the next five years of my life. She predicted I'd have two children and maybe a third later on. I'm very intuitive, she said, and this child will be, too. She repeatedly commented on my glowing good health and saw no problems for me or the baby. She kept seeing a television and wasn't sure what that meant. And she predicted that in four years, in March, I will be faced with an important decision. Not career versus family, she said, but a choice between two compelling opportunities. Sounds intriguing. Our marriage is solid and the baby very wanted. She mentioned with uncertainty that perhaps I was seeking a female friend or guide. Both ideas are true. I've been looking for local support in the form of both a close local friend (or friends) and someone to act as an editor or mentor.

What amused me greatly was that, despite my long-time interest well-tempered with cynicism, I was reassured by her reading. Pony was OK! I'd been fretting inside for five days, barely aware I was doing it, yet never fully reassured by the kicks or rolls I did feel. When I had found myself in tears on the phone with Rick the night before, I knew something was wrong. I couldn't pinpoint whether it was fear for Pony or sadness and loneliness in the face of distance from Nancy. It was probably both. And then a psychic beamingly tells me I'm in great shape and that I'll be having a girl, and all my confidence is restored? Crazy! But it happened. Since then, Pony's movements felt stronger, more pronounced.

Until the last two days. One thing is becoming more certain: the busier I am, the more involved with my own life, the less aware I become of Pony. Am I trying to cram in too much? Desperately trying to get established as a writer again Before Baby? To establish a routine, a guiding goal to return to as my baby gives me time? As I steal time from my baby? To keep my body tuned with exercise now so the habit will exist when the real work is ahead of me after birth? Will I still look pregnant while the baby lies in the crib?

Cribs! Belks called yesterday. The crib ordered only four weeks ago is in! While four weeks seems like plenty of time, they said not to expect it for 12 weeks. A little close for comfort but manageable. And now it's here! Yet to be delivered and set up, but around the corner.

And Pony's only three months away, too. October 1 (a date by which this kid should have arrived) sounds so far away. A full season. A summer. So much can happen in a summer. While in school — so many years of my life — it was a time to rejoice, to play, to recharge, to travel, to learn, to grow. So much can change in a summer. Grand expectations for autumn (or grand fears) but newness and change guaranteed with the season. All true this summer, too.

I heard from Roberta this week, too. She's been living in Canada for many years. At Christmas I learned she and Stuart were having fertility problems. This letter, while sounding cheerful, reported a miscarriage at seven weeks. After 15 months of trying. She didn't mention any involvement with a fertility program, so I assume nature had taken its course. Her letter only touched on the pain of the loss. They were on vacation, and she appreciated having two weeks after the miscarriage on the beaches of Portugal so they could recoup. Perhaps the act of conception was reaffirming to them, overpowering the loss. I'll write her soon. As I want to write Sarah. I've owed a note since Christmas when she sent me a long updating letter. Baby issues all around. Her husband, father of two teens from a prior marriage, has just reversed his vasectomy so he and Sarah can try and have children.

A phone call from my sweetie. He hadn't told me until now, but he's begun having anxiety attacks about the baby, about how the baby will change our lives and whether he'll be a good father. As he said, in marriage there's still a certain level of independence, but as a parent! So far our moments of fear have balanced. He's fine when I'm scared and visa versa. Today I could reassure him — or try to! I reminded him how we'll be there together to help each other, how we'll buy our private time together, as a couple, with sitters, how we'll each still have time alone, independent time, while we spell each other. All true, yet none, I realize, able to balance the enormity of the change ahead.

June 19

I'm turning into a shrew. It's horrible! I can only hope its my hormones, or perhaps latent anxiety — something that will dissipate. Last night I blew up at Rick for no good reason. He'd been at work most of the day, then ran. A long Saturday for him. At midday, he came home to help me take the dogs to the vet; he was late and I was irritated. Afterward, he went back to work and I spent the afternoon grocery shopping, measuring the nursery for furniture and shades, and pulling weeds. By the end of the day, I was tired. I may still have been catching up from West Coast jet lag, too.

Seven o'clock rolled around, and we were just relaxing and reading. I knew I was getting hungry but felt too tired to get dinner. Rick was reading but I expected him to be a mind reader. As 8 o'clock drew near and I had already complained a few times about fatigue, I began to feel irrationally angry. Why didn't *he* take care of *me*? Why do I have to ask him if he'll organize dinner? He finally did offer but, by then, I was so mad sitting around waiting for him to offer, I wasn't appeased.

By bedtime, after going out to see the movie *Bull Durham*, I was extremely tired and picking a fight. My back hurt, and I felt put upon that he never (it seemed) offered to do anything concrete for me. He will often ask if there's anything he can do. He usually does the dishes, he loves me and is very patient, but I felt furious that I had to ask for a back rub. I'm pregnant for Pete's sake! Aren't I supposed to get some pampering?

And today, despite sleeping late, apparently I wasn't through with my tantrum. Rick was talking to his Dad on the phone and mentioned that I'd seen the psychic on my trip, and I threw a fit. Which was stupid. He wasn't making fun of me. He was amused, as I had been, but I was pissed off now. After a brief yelling match (mostly on my part, as he was dumbfounded), I apologized, feeling like a snake. I hated myself for acting so obnoxious, yet I was still not fully convinced it was all my fault. After we played with the dogs together to further diffuse the air, I cried in his arms. That's all I really wanted anyway, to be held and cared for. Yet my behavior seemed designed to drive away what I wanted most.

Friday, over a night out of pizza and beer, we talked more about our fears. Fear of being a bad parent. Fear of not liking the job. Fear of loss of independence. Fear that Pony will die before he is born. Then, despite these fears, we spent the next hour before our movie started entertaining ourselves at Toys "Я" Us.

Such paradoxes are nothing new these days. For example, first I feel like a whale and then I look at other women who are six months pregnant and I feel I'm not big enough. Someone says, in surprise, "You don't look six months pregnant!" and I'm sure something's wrong with the baby. Rick says he thinks I'm carrying it well, and I fret to him that I'm afraid something's wrong. He says no, I'm just big-boned and have more room. And then I'm insulted and say that I'm not big-boned; I just must be fat if that's what he thinks. Am I going to feel insulted by everything for the next three months? And what of the hormone swings after that?

Help!

June 21

The bug bites on my legs are driving me crazy! Neither calamine lotion nor Sea Breeze offers more than momentary relief. This morning, I've grabbed some ice cubes. Numbing them helps.

June 22

I've been incredibly preoccupied this week, especially the last few days. It's time to decorate the nursery! The crib is here although unassembled. My attention has focused on three things: a dresser/changing table, baby bedding, and curtains. I've become frenzied with excitement and frustration. Details loom large and obstacles anger me yet fuel my fire. Why has this become so immediately all-consuming? Why am I so incredibly impatient? I want things done right, and I want them done now. I do have three months to go. Why does preparation become all-important? If the baby came within the next two months, it surely would be in the hospital a while before it came home.

I feel I'm desperately trying to prove there *will* be a baby. That nothing's going to go wrong now. That the nursery will be complete and ready. I'm being good to myself by planning to have everything desired on hand so there's no added unnecessary stress after birth. Yet there's still that quiet inner voice asking me what I'm doing. What am I going to do with a nursery full of stuff when this baby, too, doesn't make it? And I'll look so silly—the first two didn't make it. Why was I so optimistic about this one? I'll be ashamed and embarrassed on top of my grief. The past *told* you that you couldn't have a baby. Why didn't you wait and see?

Mostly that sense of worry is inaudible, merely hovering on the farthest perimeter. I worry much more about things like my selection of bedding and decor. If I buy the alphabet bears pattern, am I secretly pushing my kid to learn, to love reading and writing like I do? I'm trying hard to keep the room a happy kid's room and not impose my own adult aesthetics. I'm shocked at how sex stereotypic I am underneath. Balking at something too frilly or too cute in case it's a boy, wanting him to be content with the basics for at least a few years. And if it's a girl? I don't lean towards the more feminine designs but I become more relaxed considering puffy balloon-style curtains. I avoid pastels even though I like some of the muted rose, taupe, mauve, and blue because research shows that babies can see primary colors better. Yet I hesitate to overload the room; the child will need a sense of peace in there now and then as much as Rick and I will.

And as I get excited about the decoration, which items will look just right, I try to remember how time-limited this is. How soon this child will assert his or her own tastes — in clothes, toys, room decor. What is my corner of paradise now, to decorate at my fancy, is being turned over to this new person. It will ultimately be her domain or his corner of privacy and self-expression. It's likely to be the most personal space she'll have until she moves out of the house.

It was odd yesterday. While looking at dressers in the Carolina Baby Superstore a clerk asked me if I was having a boy or a girl. Not did I know; just which is it. When I said I didn't know, she was surprised. I detected slight condescension that I was so old-fashioned as not to opt for modern technological means to find out!

June 23

More household headaches. The electrician didn't show up yesterday; nor did the new cleaning lady. The electrician apologized and set up a new date. The cleaning person has been incommunicado so today I will begin to look for another.

Yesterday Pony was kicking a lot. Not at all uncomfortable (yet), just reassuring. This morning, too. And the night before last when we went to our first La Leche League meeting. The meeting centered on the advantages of breast-feeding. Actually, neither of us needs convincing. Rick maybe a little, simply because he'd like to be able to feed the baby, too. The only fear or potential disadvantage I can foresee is fatigue. Will the more frequent feedings exhaust me even more? Even if that's true, I haven't even considered bottle-feeding. It doesn't seem right. It seems artificial and a rejection of the child. If nature knows best in birthing, at least in normal uncomplicated births, nature knows best in feeding and nurturing, too.

But I'm nervous about the effects of fatigue on my system. Fatigue, shit, I mean basic sleep deprivation. Even if I sleep when the baby sleeps, the interruption of natural adult sleep cycles often has a devastating effect. And I get so cranky and out of sorts when I'm simply tired! I've begun reading a book called *The New Mother Syndrome* about postpartum depression. It's not scaring me, but I'm trying hard to be prepared for whatever may come my way. Some women actually become psychotic from the hormonal shifts, sleep deprivation, and life-style change. Although I'm not far into the book, it seems odd to claim that postpartum depression (PPD) can occur from a few days to a year after birth and be unrelated to breast-feeding. That knocks down the hormone argument to me. I'm hoping the fact that I already work at home and am used to being here will temper the feelings of new mother isolation.

Talking with some of the women in the prenatal exercise class yesterday made me jealous and nervous. One woman is due October 8, three weeks after me, and I look so much less pregnant. (Is there something vaguely male here . . . "mine's bigger than yours"?) She can even feel through her uterus and tell how the baby is positioned. I'll ask Linda at our next visit to show me how to do that.

Rick isn't sure, but he thinks he can hear Pony's heartbeat (faintly) when he puts his ear to my tummy. He has been able to feel some good strong movement the last few days.

The pear trees no longer look so naked; they've sprouted leaves.

June 24

I feel I'm ready to write about our experiences with Parent Care last July and August, yet I suffer from an amnesia similar to that surrounding the second miscarriage. So many details from that intense group experience have fled from memory. I wish I had been keeping my journal with more frequency during that time. I've found only three entries and they don't begin to show how powerful the experience was, how moving, how strengthening. Still, they're the best information I have to begin reexamining that period of my life.

*   *   *

July 19

Grief Support Group—Parent Care—for those who have lost children less than one year old. I was near tears throughout, but felt strengthened, and eagerly look forward to the next meeting.

One woman lost her baby, Carly, born at 32 weeks. The movements just stopped. The heartbeat was gone. The child seemed to have no defects. It just died. She was so numb, she couldn't cry. Her voice, expressionless.

Another woman rocks the urn filled with the ashes of her son every night, then kisses his picture. Born at 28 weeks, he lived 18 hours. She does this every night before she tries to sleep. She thinks she's going crazy. Can't remember how she gets home from work each day. She made a $55 million accounting error in her job. She's distracted.

Beth, who lost Lydia. Born several months premature, lived in the hospital five months, then died. A $160,000 hospital bill. All paid but an unexplained $18 worth—a bill that comes with repeated regularity. She still gets mail addressed to Lydia Hill. Sometimes Mrs. Lydia Hill. Says she's tempted to call the sender, raging at that. Lydia is dead, and what's more, Lydia was only five months old, hardly a "Mrs."

Another had a photo developer lose her baby pictures. The only pictures of her son. They finally found them. She wants to show them to people so badly but is afraid her tiny stillborn will frighten them. Or they'll be repulsed.

Another lost her baby in February. Stephen was born on time but had a deviated hernia. The boy's intestines had grown all the way into his chest because there was no wall, so his lungs weren't able to mature. When they tried to resuscitate him, his lungs popped. She had recently gone to the lake with her husband and his family, and all the images of bringing her children to visit the lake as they grew up overwhelmed her again.

Everybody cries all the time.

One large woman relies on blunt, broad humor and determinedly high spirits. She says she's cried, but I believe she's yet to cry from deep down.

One woman put her seven-year-old son's shoes in the refrigerator weeks after she lost her baby. He just shook his head and said, "Sometimes I worry about you Mom."

Beth's husband doesn't come to the group. She apologized, saying he's very supportive and loving and there for her and their son, but told her he just can't stand to be around so many sad people.

August 20

Our third night of Parent Care. Every first and third Thursday. Four weeks ago, we started. On February 13th, I miscarried our first child (at 12 1/2 weeks). On May 26th, I miscarried our second child (at 9 weeks). Last week I was afraid I was having a third miscarriage — earlier and earlier each time — but no, only a late and painful period.

We all talked about faith tonight. Or the lack thereof. I helped a woman. I actually helped a woman. Like me, she has problems accepting organized religion. For her, it's just parts of it that aren't acceptable. But she feels angry she doesn't have faith. And felt there's no way to get faith. You can't trick yourself, believing because you'll feel comforted. Yet she does have a faith in herself and in mankind. But she's afraid not to believe in Christ for fear the fundamentalist types might be right: reject Christ and go to hell. And without that certain belief, she's afraid she might never see her dead baby daughter again.

I said I thought her beliefs and those of standard religions could both be true. Her faith in mankind and herself is the same as faith in

Jesus — just a little more abstract, not relying on symbolism. So she didn't have to believe by the rules to have salvation. It makes sense to me, and it seemed to make sense to her, too.

We talked about why that doesn't help me. And I talked about the massive pain and suffering in the world. How I can accept an abstract concept of God but can't personalize it and thus can't find any comfort. She focuses within; I seem to focus without.

Rick suggested I look for that faith by looking within, loving within. Being selfish. My thought was, "Good Lord, I'm already horribly selfish!" But perhaps what I am is horribly hard on myself. Maybe I can find my personal voice with God within. Maybe.

September 2

Feeling very, very stressed. Wild-eyed and electrified about the road paving payment issues at the new house.

Trying to be kind to myself, counting the stresses of this past year, still feeling close to tears.

August '86	*sold house*
September '86	*moved*
September '86	*started new job*
October '86	*bought house*
December '86	*got pregnant*
February '87	*lost baby*
April '87	*got pregnant*
May '87	*lost baby*
June '87	*became responsible for my trust fund*
August '87	*left job*
August '87	*sold house*
September '87	*moved*
October '87	*bought house*

A very stressful year. Leaving a job is supposed to be one way to reduce stress and hopefully it will. I don't love the job and I don't want that commute, but I fear I'm walking into extreme isolation.

I'm trying to take deep breaths and stroke myself for my resil-

*ience, my flexibility. I've done unusual things most of my life.
Change is always an opportunity for growth. True, but right now I
feel overgrown . . . spiky and untended.*

* * *

The meetings saw us through. They didn't solve everything; they
didn't erase our wounds. They did open doors. Throw us ropes.
Extend safety nets. Rick and I marveled. How could a group of
such incredibly diverse people, unlikely even to know each other
much less be friends, come together with such intimacy?

We said throughout the summer that we'd continue with the
group after our move, commuting from Orange County to Raleigh.
We didn't. Sometimes I think we should still go back. Of course,
our losses haunt this pregnancy. Maybe talking some more would
help.

We didn't return, under the pretense of settling in. We *were*
busy, and disoriented. But I think we really didn't go back because
somehow we believed our new house would give us a new start, a
clean slate. No more bad memories, no more bad luck.

June 27

A bizarre dream last night. Our neighbors began constructing a
fence on our land. Not just a little ways over the line but about 40
feet onto our property. They knew it was our land, too. I was furious. I wanted something done immediately—lawyers called—or to
simply go and remove it!

This dream, at this point, is an extension of reality. We've been
on eggshells with the neighbors since we moved in. Their driveway
encroaches on our land a good distance, and we've worked out an
exchange of land so they can own their driveway and we can have
the acreage we bargained for. However, due mostly to the centipede
speed of our mortgage company, this deal is yet to be finalized but
the assumption is that we all agree. The dream began here with their
flaunting of the agreement.

My fury seemed to know no bounds yet I felt helpless. Sitting in
the bedroom, I grabbed a magazine (which turned out to be a baby

catalogue) and stabbed at it viciously, repeatedly with a red-ink pen, cutting deep puncture wounds.

This anger could be tied to many things. The previous evening I failed, again, at lovemaking. This has never been a problem before, but my interest has waned recently. Regardless of our position I feel discomfort. It must be distracting me too much. And I'm left feeling frustrated and awkward at not being able to better communicate my needs.

My nesting instinct flew into full swing this weekend. I spent Saturday afternoon cleaning out the garage. It's much improved! Throwing out boxes and boxes of trash and resorting boxes of memories, pitching some of those, was cathartic. This mass exodus of junk, along with some good items to be picked up by Goodwill, allows us to actually use the garage for cars. What a novel idea! This will be particularly nice when the baby comes, so we won't have to walk outside in the rain to get the kid in the car.

Jessie, our basset, infuriated me today. I put her and Bruin in the fenced yard because the electrician was due. (Of course, four hours later, he's still not here.) She barked and barked and continued to raise a huge fuss. I got irritated because it's a gorgeous day: cool, blue sky, low humidity (so pleasant after yesterday's 100 degrees with 90 percent humidity). After 45 minutes of racket, with occasional silences in response to my shouts out the window of "No Bark!" I heard silence. Then I heard the tell-tale slap of the second screened door from the porch.

She had clawed through the wood moldings that held the plexiglass screen cover (in place to prevent her from scratching through the screen), causing the cover to slip to the ground. She then sashayed through the torn screen and nosed her way through the other door.

Half an hour of hammering made the door block functional again but who knows for how long now that she's learned? How has she gotten so spoiled? Us, I realize, but why does she hate the yard so? She's been in fenced yards her entire life!

Poor Bruin is too timid to go through either the hole or the second door. Jessie, by contrast, is a bulldozer.

June 29

How long did the door last? One day. Yesterday morning she broke out again. This time only able to remove part of the wood molding (the nails held a little), she actually broke the plexiglass and, of course, the screen. I dashed in at noon, after a four-hour wait for Rick's car, to check on the electricians. And there she was, sauntering around like she owned the place, ambling up and down with the workers. They had, fortunately, brought her inside. I can't believe she did that! I also can't believe she didn't hurt herself. I kept her in the rest of the day with only supervised visits to the yard.

By 9 o'clock last night Rick and I had finished a more substantial repair job. Just as the spinach-ricotta pie was ready for dinner. So far, so good. She's been quieter today with only one spate of frenzied barking. This time my sharp "No!" quieted her down, unless she's already escaped again and I missed it!

Yesterday was like a roller coaster. Not enough sleep, crazy hormones. The night before, I got annoyed at Rick (which seems to be happening a lot lately). Car problems have plagued us for months. The Bronco has been stalling, bucking, bouncing, and bursting in and out with a schizophrenic radio speaker. Rick had taken it to a recommended repair shop last month. They estimated $250, charged $500, and didn't fix anything. I wanted him to have them explain the jacked up bill and actually *fix* the car now. When he finally talked to them about it, they just gave him some useless explanations of the charges and claimed things either had been fixed or couldn't be fixed any further without costing a lot more money. This is not a satisfactory answer to me.

So, yesterday I took the car into another repair place and waited and fumed for four hours. I felt he should have been tougher (and angrier) with the first repair shop. And I resented waiting around for *his* car to be fixed. What do I resent more: actually taking charge of his car or the fact that my work, my writing, seems less and less important? Certainly my schedule is more flexible, but I feel myself slipping more and more into some housewifely role. Open to others' stereotyped expectations and fearing those assumptions will materialize in full and the rest of my identity will be lost. But surely housewife is part of my identity. I don't mind that. I enjoy putting the house together, making it comfortable and appealing. It's the maintenance stuff that's no fun.

All these tensions pervaded Monday and Tuesday. Fatigue dogged both Rick and me. We seem to fall into a quiet competitiveness with underlying surliness: "I had such a bad day I deserve more care and thoughtfulness from my mate." Kind of tricky when that's the hidden agenda of both parties.

Monday night was our first childbirth preparation class. I arrived home at 7:00 p.m. from exercise class. We had to leave between 7:30 and 7:45. Given that departure time, I expected Rick to be home by then so we could grab a bite together. Nope. He came in at 7:20. It turns out that his only goal was to make it home by 7:30. Again, I was annoyed. An unvoiced expectation? Did I actually *say*, "Let's plan to eat together at 7:00?" Probably not. Was I able to balance my feelings with that fact at the time? No. Still, we hugged and agreed to be friends again before we went out the door.

The class was fine. It will be just us which is both good and bad. We'll certainly get individualized attention, but I'll miss the camaraderie of working with other couples. Jenny seems to be a good instructor although she also seemed nervous during the first class. She's a therapist and appeared to be holding back her own personality in a classic counselor mode to encourage us to be forthcoming. I hope she changes that. I want her to be spontaneous, too.

The first class consisted of general medical background information and sharing of feelings and expectations. We saw a video of five births. The variety of responses from the new Moms was fun to see. All were intensely emotional after the birth. This felt right. I remember last year when we talked to Mike and Annette half an hour after Patrick was born. Mike was excited but Annette sounded just the same, like it was no big deal!

Monday night, after Rick had fallen asleep, I lay in bed reading and Pony became incredibly active. I think she had the hiccups, but she was also kicking and turning. Some sort of movement also caused a sharp pain. It happened several times and has occurred a couple of times since to a lesser extent. I don't think they were Braxton-Hicks contractions. I think I've already felt those and they're different — a tightening of the abdomen. This pain is centered in my lower uterus, in the front. It's very sharp and sudden, lasting only a few seconds, but it feels like a raw nerve. Like when the dentist is drilling and hits an exposed nerve. It just shoots straight through me, a vibrating, lacerating pain. I'll ask the midwife about it. I assume it's normal but my body involuntarily jerks and tenses at the sensation. If that's only imitation labor, how will I consciously relax during the real thing?

I had a baby dream this morning. I was home with the newly born child. Its appearance kept changing. Generally, it was tiny, the size of my finger or my hand, and it looked like a cloth doll. All this was perfectly normal in the dream. The problem was changing its diapers. The little thing was diapered but pooping to beat the band. The baby and I were having a conversation about its poop and how I would change its diapers, but I didn't have the nursery organized. I wasn't sure where to perform this cleanup function. Throughout the dream the size of the baby kept changing yet it all seemed matter-of-fact.

July 1

I can't believe it. After a day of extreme contrition from Jessie, mooning around, nuzzling, hand licking, and lap sitting, she pooped in the baby's room! Right in the middle of the floor. I don't know if she just needed to go and it seemed like an out-of-the-way spot (unlikely), she's mad at us, or she senses something different happening in that room. It's slowly changing—old curtains down, fixtures up, crib in—and I spend more time there (with a measuring tape or just staring).

At the pool today I chatted with two other pregnant women, friends who swim together. They, too, are due at the end of September. When they found I had the same due date, they groaned at their bodies and said I was so little and/or they felt so big. I told them I alternated in feeling like a whale and feeling I was too small, that something must be wrong.

But today's midwife visit dispelled that fear. My uterine growth is right on target. The baby is lying diagonally with its head on my upper right side and feet on the lower left. At least that's how it was at 2 o'clock!

I heard some disturbing news this morning from my pregnant cohorts at the pool. It was confirmed on my afternoon visit with Ruth. The second midwife, Linda, left the practice. Yesterday was her last day. Rick and I talked extensively to Ruth about it. Ruth has been a midwife with these doctors for many years. Linda had just started in the fall. Officially I don't know why Linda left. My pool contacts said she was having health problems—an old knee injury couldn't tolerate a weight-bearing job. Ruth, a bit tight-lipped, didn't say; she only indicated Linda didn't give a lot of notice.

Ruth promised she would be available to deliver her patients but noted that she would be taking a week off for a conference starting October 12. I certainly should have delivered by then, but I'm still nervous. I've heard of people being three weeks late. I don't want my labor to be arbitrarily induced, and I don't want to deliver with a doctor if there's no medical need. Certainly I'll deliver before October 12th!

The other concern I carry, which she did not fully address, is her actual availability during labor. She agreed that the patient load is heavier than when she was practicing without Linda, but she said she's never missed a baby. She's had three women in labor at the same time and delivered babies five minutes apart.

I'm not reassured by that description. All she's done is convince me that she'll be there to catch the kid. But one of the reasons I chose a midwife was to have more personalized attention and support through the entire birthing process. If Ruth has to bounce from room to room while I'm in transition, I won't be getting what I bargained for.

One option is to switch practices which I'm not eager to do. Another option would be to hire a doula (an extra labor coach) to supplement Rick. Jenny, our Bradley teacher, is an obvious possibility, but I have some doubts. I need to talk more with Ruth. For example, I'd like to know how many of her patients are due between September 12th and 28th. It seems like a fair question to me, but I suddenly feel nervous about alienating her. It's frustrating, as I felt closer to Linda anyway. I have been concerned about Ruth all along. In the few appointments I've had with her, she's seemed harried and tired. I've presumed its due to the added stress in her personal life. She just had a son in March. She can't be getting all the sleep she needs. Today, though, despite having a woman in labor somewhere, she was more relaxed than earlier visits.

I had two vials of blood drawn for standard tests: a diabetes screen and an Rh titer. The latter is to ensure that my blood hasn't become sensitized against an Rh + baby. Assuming it hasn't, I will get a prophylactic shot of RhoGAM. If my blood has sensitized, my pregnancy becomes high risk. My blood pressure is 100 over 57 and I've gained 18 pounds.

Ruth assured us the chances of delivery as early as August 6th (when Rick will be away for the weekend) are extremely slim. She said that even if I did go into labor, they would do everything they could to stop it. Delivery before 36 weeks isn't considered safe.

I'm beginning my third trimester!

The shooting pains I felt earlier this week are normal, too. She said the belly button area has many nerves, as do a few other locations in there. Such pains may come and go. Some women feel them, some don't.

The chair for my office, the book-lined space across the hall from our bedroom, arrived today. I now have a completed space of my own.

July 5

Three dreams in the last three days.

This morning I dreamt I birthed five or six babies. They were so small that they were likely to die. Each was the size of my hand. I was terrified they would die and furious at the midwife. She should have known. They had assured me I wasn't even carrying twins! If they'd known, we could have protected them better.

Yesterday I dreamt I was nursing the dogs, literally, at my breast. The baby had been born, but my milk hadn't come in. So Jessie and Bruin and a third puppy that looked like a baby Bruin suckled at my breasts till my milk came in.

When I told Rick this one, he asked if the baby was a boy or a girl, and I realized I didn't know. The baby appeared briefly in the dream (it had dark hair) but that was it. The rest was nursing the dogs.

Finally, a third dream. Very disorienting and upsetting. We were moving, *again*! Leaving this house. I didn't even know why. Rick was completely absent from the dream. My brothers lived here instead. I was panicking. I kept ticking off everything I'd done for the house in the last few months, thinking it all such an utter waste. Purchased rugs, installed fixtures and garage door openers, bought some furniture, hung pictures . . . got it just right and created a home. And now we were moving out that day. Packing, movers arriving. "Why?" I kept asking. "We don't need to move. We promised we'd stay. We really like it here!"

My brothers and I were also going on vacation somewhere before arriving at our new home. We were taking my car. I still had my Honda Civic, my "single person" car. I began to panic at that, too. I needed to fill the car with items that couldn't go in the moving van: plants, suitcases, etc. How could the three of us, all our vacation gear, and the two dogs also fit in? I successfully persuaded them to rent a car.

Several little old ladies I didn't know came by to help with the packing. I continued to feel upset and helpless.

Finally I walked outside and the dream shifted to a level of lucid dreaming, a minimal awareness that this was a dream. I told the movers, "I've changed my mind, we're not moving," fully expecting it to have no effect. But I had told myself, "This is too strange. There's no reason to move. It must be a dream." And, indeed, they said, "OK, Lady," and started unpacking. I felt great relief as I awoke.

Was this another will-baby-destroy-family dream? My brothers representing my birth family? The house being dismantled representing the utter change and possible chaos around the corner?

Aside from my dream world, things have been fairly normal although I still react oddly to certain snippets of life. My body, aside from the obvious, is not on an even keel. I seem to attract biting insects. I've suffered more bites at once than I recall ever getting before. And each bite results in a more extreme reaction than ever before, a larger area of redness and swelling that takes longer to recede.

My identity continues to ride in flux. One of the women at the pool asked me, "When are you due?" I thought she asked "What do you do?" and thus responded that I worked at home as a writer. She gave me a quizzical look and repeated her original question. It's especially amusing to me because I recall once, much earlier in my pregnancy, the opposite mistake occurring. Another woman asked what I did, and I responded with equal subsequent embarrassment, "The end of September."

A pleasant evening last night nonetheless gave me another excuse to worry about Pony. We went with Becky and Randy to hear the North Carolina Symphony and to see the fireworks at Regency Park. A picnic under the pines, relaxed and soothed. Good food, good humor, good people-watching. Lots of talk about pregnancy and the baby.

When the fireworks exploded, I expected a reaction from Pony. She'd been quiet all day, and the noise was fierce. Pony turned over or stretched maybe twice at the beginning, and that was it. I told myself the peace was due to my swaying with the accompanying music. This must be soothing the baby, or the womb insulated Pony from the noise more than I thought. Or that Pony's gonna love fireworks and loud noise — a very placid baby. Besides, the explosions only made *me* startle a few times.

Regardless, I didn't convince myself of anything. I felt sure that something was wrong and that Pony was growing weaker. Perhaps he's Rh+ and my blood has developed antibodies and is attacking him. . . .

Today that fear is thankfully out the window. The Rh titer test, the glucose screen, and the urine culture all came back normal. My urine is bacteria-free (no infection), my glucose is 109 (135 is the cutoff, so no developing diabetes), and the Rh screen is negative (no antibodies).

July 6

I was with another person, by a lake, ready to swim. I don't know who this person was; I don't even know if the person was a male or a female. But we entered the water to swim partway around the lake. When we got in, we discovered there was a tide or a current forcing us back, preventing us from swimming where we wanted to go. Eventually we found a channel in the middle. There was no wind or current pushing us back. There, while watching for boats and ready to move out of their way, we swam swiftly, unencumbered.

July 8

I'm feeling large. Not just my tummy. That area is finally beginning to feel large enough (with people beginning to recognize I'm pregnant). My hips and legs feel fat. What caused this mental transformation? First, catching a glimpse of myself in a mirror at prenatal exercise class on Wednesday and then being filmed with our video camera last night. The first of a series beginning pre-Pony. I even volunteered, suggested to Rick that it might be a good night. I was feeling more put together than normal at the end of the day, but what an illusion. I looked and sounded terrible. Oh well, maybe later I'll look back and laugh. Rick came out great, and so did the dogs. Especially Jessie. Ms. Photogenic.

The Bradley class is fine. I understand the importance of nutrition and respect that emphasis, but I find it hard to get up to 100 grams of protein per day. Still, some of her suggestions are helpful. They're things I've known but recently failed to do: keep hard-boiled eggs handy and doctor food with wheat germ and sunflower seeds. Drinking a full quart of milk per day isn't that easy either, but I get the extra calcium from all the cheese I eat. At least proper eating encourages me to withdraw from sweets — there isn't enough room for both!

We talked with Rick's Dad last night. He wanted to know how

much weight I've gained, how I felt, whether the baby is keeping me up at night with kicking. The last made me wonder again. *Should* Pony's kicking be stronger? Is everything really OK in there? Recalling Ruth's questions: "Feeling lots of good strong fetal movement?" Am I? What is "good strong fetal movement"? What does it feel like? How often should I feel it? The only thing that wakes me up is a 4:00 a.m. need to pee. I do and am immediately out like a light.

And Richard, my father-in-law, says, with all seriousness, "I want you to take care of that baby." Good Lord, what does he think I'm doing? I know he means it in the kindest way, but I do all that I can that's good for me and avoid everything that might be bad for me, and the whole damn thing is still out of my hands.

I talked with Elaine Wednesday night. She, like Rob and Pete, insisted I get some pictures taken. I laughed and said I'd been at Rick to do it but he hadn't. She pointed out that I have the tripod and could do it myself. So I replaced the dead batteries in my camera yesterday and will attempt some self-portraits.

During the last few days everything seems slowed down. My energy and activities since April seem to be fading away, yet I can't figure out exactly what's happening or why. Well, the why is surely the natural increase of fatigue in the final leg of this journey. But the what? I've started sleeping later in the morning and then just piddling around until it's time to swim at noon, not getting to my desk at all, spending time I don't know where.

I'm also a bit down because I'm feeling socially isolated, lonely. I felt put-upon and rejected (totally irrationally) while in Belk's yesterday. I love Irene, the saleslady who's been helping me, but inside I was bemoaning my lack of community support here. Belk's has a baby shower gift registry service. And yesterday there were several women in there buying for their pregnant friends. And all I could think was that I don't even know if my *family* members are going to get us anything. Nobody (at least on my side) has asked what we need. There's no one to register for. No one will be giving us a baby shower. It's all true, but I believe I'm engaging in what one woman in my prenatal class called a pity party.

July 11

I'm clearly beginning to feel the effects of later pregnancy however amorphous. I have few discernible aches or pains but frequently feel ill at ease with my body. I notice it more as I grow tired
at the end of the day. All the heaviness in my lower belly. Not being
completely comfortable no matter how I sit. Unable to bend over to
wash my face, feeling awkward trying to reach the sink with a squat
or modified plié. I am, thankfully, still comfortable sleeping at
night once I get settled. I do tend to wake up for a middle-of-the-
night trip to the toilet and to half wake when I turn over, but I fall
asleep again almost immediately.

I feel my anxiety about being a parent rising again. In those
groggy moments when I stumble to the bathroom, I always think,
"Oh God, I'm going to have to actually *do* things at such an un-
heard of hour." I won't be able to snooze through the quick rote
motion of a few steps out of bed and back again. Maybe breast-
feeding can become that routine, but diaper changing? And com-
forting a baby who needs to cry? There's no question that will de-
mand something of me. Often, a lot of me. My largest fear? How
am I going to be able to go without sleep?

I am seriously thinking about one child: this is it. I realize that I
hardly need to decide that now, but with so much required of one to
do it well and so many other competing activities in our adult lives,
one child seems just fine. But how much would Pony miss having a
brother or sister?

Rick put the crib together yesterday. It looks great. And self-
doubt flooded me again. The best place for the crib is in the far left
corner. The room's so small there aren't a lot of options. But Rick
was concerned that the air vent in the ceiling would blow right on
the baby. It didn't seem like it would to me, but he was still concerned. An adjustment to the vent sent the air toward the center of
the room and he relaxed. Yet afterwards I felt insensitive. I wasn't
worried about drafts on the baby? What kind of mother would I be!

My dreams have become more violent. The details evade me.
Two nights ago, I was a passenger in a car. A convertible? Sud-

denly something very small struck me in the upper stomach with a great deal of velocity. I had a puncture wound. I thought it might have been a piece of gravel but pressure to the sides of the wound brought something to the surface: a pencil point consisting of the graphite tip and perhaps 3/4 of an inch. The rest had broken off somewhere before impact.

Last night I dreamt of stabbings. Women. I was one. Sometimes I seemed interchangeable with another. I don't think I knew any of them. There were no men. In parts, I was fleeing or being stabbed; in other parts, I had the knife. At one moment, near the end, a blond woman was stabbed, and the act of stabbing (something magical or inherent in the knife) immediately aged her into an old woman.

July 15

My sleep has continued to be filled with bizarre and confusing dreams. I'm unable to remember most of them and, when I do, they are too fragmented to explain. My parents appear with regularity. The focus is on my mother but my father is usually there. It's strange — I've had so few dreams about him in the 12 years since his death and now he's there all the time. I recall that after he died I wished I would dream about him more often, but I only had a handful. I thought they'd help explore the feelings I had to deal with at that time. Instead, I had to struggle through the conscious layers to resolve the unresolved. Now he's there with my Mom, as if he never died. A background figure. Do I not want to grow up . . . leaving my birth family intact, untouched and unchanged?

Usually there is some tension in the dreams of my mother. In one dream it was Thanksgiving in the house in New Jersey. Mom was hosting the holiday. No other relatives were there yet but she hadn't set a place for me. She was not at all contrite. I either wasn't expected or wasn't invited.

Then this morning there was another dream about Mom and her mother, Grandma Esther, who has been dead four years now. I was close to that grandmother as a child but pulled away from her as an adolescent. This was partly because I pulled away from everyone then and partly because I sensed the long-brewing tension between my mother and her mother. In this dream fragment I was observer, not participant. Gram was having intestinal problems and giving herself enemas. Mom was displeased. Gram, though not very healthy, was neither fragile, dependent, nor contrite.

Sometimes I feel I am not cut out to be a mother. I'm not talking to Pony. In everything I read, pregnant women at least *occasionally* have conversations with their in utero charge. I feel I'm pulling back emotionally. That I was more involved in the second trimester.

I was in the Regulator bookstore a few days ago and browsed through a book on pregnancy loss. I sat there for 15 minutes reading a woman's account of her stillbirth. It reminded me of Parent Care. Everything had gone great during pregnancy. She was at her last scheduled appointment before the baby was due. And the doctor couldn't find a heartbeat. Instead of inducing her, they waited for her to deliver. Three days, carrying a baby she knew had died. For no reason. The autopsy never even revealed a reason. He just died.

July 18

Saturday I realized I was terrified. Really afraid of having the baby. Not labor or birth but having a child in the house. Ours. Our responsibility. My responsibility. The feeling has been brewing for a while. Even recognizing it Saturday didn't ease it because it poked itself into my conscious in tandem with guilt. I *can't* have any real doubts about this baby. That will jinx the pregnancy for sure. I've lost and grieved over two, and it's taken so long to get here. How can I have any doubts or regrets about the choice to parent! To be afraid I won't enjoy raising a child, not enjoy it at all, is heresy.

At first I couldn't even tell Rick, but by late Saturday night I talked. A little, anyway. We had joined some friends for a casual dinner with their assortment of children ranging in age from 15 months to seven years. There was nothing wrong with any of these kids—basically they were well behaved. So why was it that all I could notice was the increased noise level, the constant interruptions, fledgling conversations continually aborted? Either a verbal child would barge in with statements or discoveries of his own or a baby would wail when a toy disappeared or Mom stepped out of sight. I also couldn't miss the food on the floor and paste on the face. It's all so *messy*, was all I could think.

Everyone, all the time, says life is never the same again. Parents talk about how amazed they are that sexual stereotypes are true. They are shocked that after working so hard at nonsexist child rearing, Tilly will slam shut the book about trucks and insist on wearing pink or Tommy will beg for toy guns, using sticks as substitutes if denied his desire. One woman insisted that no matter what career path the mother actually followed, the children always seek career advice from their Dads. Will I be assaulted with such stereotypes from within the home as well as from without? Will it really not matter *what* I do? I think I could live with my child choosing a stereotypic role, but for her to perpetually assume that it is the only correct or proper choice would curl my hair.

But that's a tangent, leading away from my gut fears. At heart, I worry about no time alone, no independence, no time for personal interests or activities, no time with my husband, no time to exercise, no time for anything but this needy creature! Ever! Rick had to pry it out of me. I'd say, "No time for me," as if that explained it all (which to me it does) but he'd press for details. He insisted we'll be able to find sitters to help and that it's important that we do since we don't have any family around to pitch in. Now, I don't disagree but all I could think was, here's yet another headache. I'll be spending double time and energy trying to line up a few people with experience whom we can trust, to buy myself a few hours at a time. It will be my responsibility to ensure that Pony will be well cared for. Rick proclaims his involvement, a desire to be in the thick of it, to come home early so I may go out, yet his actual activities convince me it won't happen. I hope I'm wrong.

These weekend terrors tell me my resilience is fading. Increased sleep has helped. While I'm not in the extreme fatigue of the first few months, I'm more easily tired. My body wants more rest. The easiest way for me to get it is to sleep late in the morning.

A dream early Sunday morning amused and comforted me, smoothing away some of my fear of being fragmented and overwhelmed. I was driving to an airport. My baby was recently born and with me in the car. I had four large suitcases in the back. The unfamiliar airport stretched on endlessly. I was looking for United Airlines (an airline I never fly, so I take the subconscious selection at symbolic face value). I was driving around a long time, searching for United and then a parking place. I finally found one curbside, a block and a half from the terminal. I put the baby in a back carrier and had to keep adjusting her as she flopped a bit from side to side. The challenge was the suitcases. How was I going to get them to the terminal? I experimented with picking them up in different ways. It was impossible to carry them all at once with the baby, too.

An older woman was walking by and I asked if she could watch two cases while I took the others to the terminal. She was happy to oblige. When I reached United, I was thrilled to see a long line of wheeled baggage carts. I hadn't even thought of them! I put my suitcases on one, wheeled it back to the car, stowed the rest of my luggage and, with my baby on my back, smoothly made my passage to United.

July 21

Where to begin? Calling it a crisis sounds too overblown, melodramatic. But yesterday it felt like a full-blown crisis, and today is not a lot better. From the beginning? Rick and I had agreed from the start that if we were to have children, we'd raise them as Jews.

Rick is a committed Reform Jew. What this translates to for our day-to-day living has been attending services on the high holidays of Rosh Hashana and Yom Kippur and occasionally going to Friday night services. We have been members of whichever temple is in our area for the last three years, although we haven't yet joined the Durham congregation. We've discussed trying to attend Friday evening services once a month but haven't reached that frequency or consistency.

I was raised without religious training. My father was a Jew who, in adult life, considered himself an atheist, lived by the Golden Rule, and never set foot inside a temple or synagogue (that I'm aware of) since we were born. My mother was raised a Catholic and walked out of the church when she was 16. She was an agnostic. We were not exposed to Catholicism or Judaism. As a child I realized that many of my friends went to Sunday school. I think I appreciated not having to go. As a teenager, I grew curious about different religions and sporadically attended a variety of services with friends. I felt a slight longing for a sense of community yet was not comfortable with the dogma of any institutionalized form of spirituality. They all struck me as too restrictive and narrow-minded. Yet I have thought for a long time that I might have benefited from being able to reject some specific religion, if rejection of organized religion was still the path I needed to follow.

So, when the question of raising our own children arose, I had no problem with Rick's desire to raise any children as Jews. I had no conflicting or alternative faith. Rick strongly identified with Judaism. I wanted to raise them "something," so our problems were solved before they began.

Until yesterday.

To be fair, a question had been brewing for a few months. It simply was not the enormous cavern of question and doubt that was ripped to the fore yesterday. The question initially took the form: if it's a boy, will we have him circumcised? This arose in March. I raised it. Circumcision was my expectation but more recent medical knowledge and current trends deem it unnecessary. To simply unthinkingly have it done seemed slightly barbaric. I cringed at inflicting such unnecessary pain on a newborn. Rick was willing, after a while, to discuss it and read some medical articles. We reached a compromise. We'd have a local anesthetic used and have the procedure done as soon as possible. We had been told that one of the doctors in our OB practice, Mike Fried, could do a modified *brit* on the eighth day of life as outlined in Jewish law. Rick was interested but agreed to prompt, unceremonious, medical removal. Issue decided.

As we sporadically attended the Friday night services these past months, our talk about religion deepened. Invariably, I would feel frustrated, defensive, and even angry at things the local rabbi preached. Rick, too, found him and the service very conservative yet still found spiritual replenishment in the familiar words and setting. I raised unanswerable questions about God. Rick tried to argue my points but was left, at his core, with only a certain level of faith. Period. A personal faith that eludes me.

My discontent was pushed to the action point when the rabbi lectured the congregation on how good Jews must strongly urge their children to date and marry only other Jews. Obviously, this didn't sit too well with Rick either. Rick suggested we sit down and talk with the rabbi. Share our views.

My angst was aggravated by the fact of Pony. Was *this* the sort of thing they'd be teaching our child in Sunday school? That was unacceptable. In fact, all my reactions to the services were enhanced by Pony's impending presence. Nobody's asking me to change, I thought. And if they are, I'm a formed, strong adult who can make her own decisions. This kid is going to be malleable. Is Pony going to be taught things I actively disagree with? I had presumed Sunday school entailed teaching a child history and tradition, prayers and ceremonies.

Rick and I finally reached a point in our discussions where I felt more comfortable. Of course our own views won't change. Of course we will answer the child honestly when she raises questions. Of course we will be honest about our own doubts, our own differences. Again, crisis averted.

In the interim this spring, I have taken a few miniature steps to investigate the Unitarian Universalist Church. A church with an almost Moonies-sounding name that is, in fact, extremely liberal, creed-free, and action-oriented. I had heard of it in Charleston; several reporters and at least one editor were members. The bits I learned then sounded interesting. So did the Quaker faith. At the time, I did nothing further.

This spring a friend from the feminist "Goddesses" class mentioned it again. The discussions of spirituality occurring in the class (the unfulfilling, patriarchal nature of most institutionalized religion), my increasing uneasiness with the rabbi at Judea Reform, and my growing need to feel that I am part of a community: all caused me to call the UUs. I only talked with an office worker. I wanted to know about their services, things I could read. She put me on their mailing list for monthly bulletins and sent a couple of background pamphlets with a list of books. This was at the end of April. I didn't attend my first service until July 10th. What I read intrigued me. I knew I was in no position to make judgements. I had only a minuscule amount of information but I felt drawn in and at home. The UUs embrace such a wide range of beliefs and expressions of spirituality. The integrating force is day-to-day commitment to justice and social action.

Rick went with me to UU services on the 10th and again on the 17th. He seemed very resistant that first morning (even though I left it open to him whether to attend) albeit expressing my desire that he keep me company. The source of tension was clear by the time we were in the car driving over. Was I balking on how we would raise the children? No. As long as we were open in the household about our differences, a program of Jewish Sunday school education was what we'd agreed on and what they'd get. He relaxed.

The service on the 10th was heavenly for me. UUs give their ministers summer sabbaticals, so a guest minister from New York was there. The theme, "A Gift of Summer," was contemplative and open-ended. She talked about the importance of slowing down, identifying your values, and acting in concert. She read a passage from one of my favorite authors, May Sarton, and mentioned that Sarton is an active Unitarian. This news felt serendipitous. Maybe I had stumbled into a spiritual home.

The next Sunday featured a political science professor who spoke for People for the American Way, an organization created to counter the Moral Majority. They fight censorship and defend the right of all groups, including the fundamentalists, to say and argue publicly what they wish. While the service was more classroom-like and less contemplative, I still enjoyed it. Feeling at one with people of like mind, of *thinking*, questioning, like minds.

Rick feels comfortable with the people and what was said, but it does not feed him spiritually. To him, it's not religion; it's a social action group. He teases about the basic lack of formalized ritual and says maybe it should be described as religious anarchy.

In between the two services, Rick finally called the rabbi to get us an appointment. Spurred on, I'm sure, by my actually getting up on a Sunday morning and going to a church service.

Each Sunday, in its entirety, was quite pleasant despite the heat. Instead of sleeping half the day and shuffling around in night-clothes with the Durham Sunday paper until midafternoon, we drove to Chapel Hill to indulge in french toast and waffles, and eggs Benedict and pancakes. We supplemented the *Morning Herald* with the *New York Times*, browsed in the bookstores, and took a Sunday drive. This still left plenty of time for lazy lounging at home with the papers. Are we up to the big day of crisis yet? All this is an attempt to organize my thoughts and put things in perspective.

At 10:00 a.m. we were walking into the rabbi's office, and by noon I was weeping over a cup of untouched chili.

What, exactly, did we go in there for anyway? Rick was upset after he made the appointment. His conversation only confirmed the rabbi's conservatism. He told me then that he was afraid the meeting might only make things worse. I was the calming note saying that, at worst, we'd just know we didn't like the rabbi. We didn't agree with him. Might there not be another rabbi within a few years anyway? Unlikely, Rick said, as this couple is well established here, as his wife is a physician. Well, I said, the rabbi need not dictate our values. We'll just talk to him.

By the time we arrived, I had decided I would play it by ear, perhaps saying very little. I know I get intense when discussing religion, and I knew there was little to be gained by sounding confrontational. My buttons got pushed almost immediately and I talked. Long before the meeting's close at 11:30, it became confrontational.

He began by saying Rick had said I was upset by some things he had said about interfaith marriage. I immediately said that the discomfort had been joint. Perhaps that is exactly where things got out of hand. I should have closed my mouth and made Rick speak. While he murmured agreement, it became my battle. It shouldn't have. We went there together.

The rabbi, a young man of 38 and obviously not some throwback conservative of two generations ago, started bolstering his points with statistics. He believes what he does about interfaith marriages because most children of interfaith marriages do not remain with the Jewish faith. The number of Jewish people is shrinking. It's his job and his calling to try to preserve the people.

In an extremely unorganized fashion, I geared many of my comments and questions toward trying to share my frustrations with organized religion in general. But, of course, I used some specifics from the services we had attended. I mentioned the sexism, and the rabbi missed the point entirely. He said, of course, in this day and age, it doesn't have to be pointed out how such practices (such as fathers and husbands annulling women's vows) are archaic. They were true at a point in history. My need to place history in present day context? Services are not classrooms, he said.

I volunteered the fact that while Rick would be disappointed if our child did not remain with the Jewish faith as an adult, I didn't have a preference one way or another. This child is going to make up his or her own mind as an adult anyway, and nothing we can do will change that. If we push too hard, we're likely to drive the child away from a faith. And yes, I agreed that children are very susceptible to peer pressure. The rabbi feels that if we are not firmly committed to raising the child as a Jew, the child will strongly resist being in a minority and won't follow through. He interpreted my comment about the child's adult decision as lack of commitment. Our commitment to send the child through a course of schooling, grades K through nine, seems as strong a commitment as you can get. You can't brainwash the child. She will go to those classes whether she wants to or not. The choice and decisions I refer to will occur in adulthood.

Yet the rabbi seemed to feel that Rick and I weren't communicating, that we had a lot to discuss. Mainly, it seemed, because I was blasé as to what religion, if any, the child may chose as an adult.

Then the rabbi stirred more information into the pot. Things, Rick said later, he never knew. At least things that he didn't know in such detail. Because my mother is not Jewish and I was not raised a Jew, I am not Jewish. I knew this (although Rick told me long ago that he felt a step closer to me because my father was Jewish). Since I am not a Jew (even though I'm not officially designated anything else), our marriage is considered an interfaith one.

We also knew that approximately 70 percent of the Jewish community will never consider our children Jews unless they actively convert (or I do). But the rabbi said even the remaining 30 percent (Reform Jews who accept patrilineal descent) would *only* consider our children Jews if several ceremonies are undertaken in addition to regular Sunday school. The child must be blessed by the rabbi on the eighth day of life, and a boy must be circumcised at that time. The child must be bar or bat mitzvahed at 13 and later confirmed. I think there were a few other points, but these are what registered. If, the rabbi said, these public declarations did not occur, "no Jew would consider the child Jewish" unless he converted. And, he added, the ritual of conversion is traumatic for youngsters.

"Exposing the child to Judaism," as he described my view of how we would raise Pony, would be entirely insufficient. We had to make a very strong commitment which, in his view, I have not made, or the child will be saying, "I'm half Jewish" or "My father's Jewish but my mother's not." The flaw in this, the rabbi continued, is not only that the child will not raise Jewish children himself but that the child will be very confused and troubled with such "ambivalent" upbringing.

God, but that makes me angry! Does that imply that I grew up confused and troubled?

Why do I resist the extra rituals? Mainly because they embody the essence of my discontent with organized religion: actions and words done and said simply because of tradition. How can I not feel angry with a faith that's telling me, no matter *what* your child *believes*, she won't be accepted as one of us unless these specific rituals are done.

I mentioned that Rick and I have a Christmas tree each year and celebrate that holiday, albeit in a secular manner. It represents love, kindness, sharing, family, doing for others and, yes, my own family tradition. I pointed out that Rick's family also routinely celebrated Christmas. The rabbi hates Christmas trees in Jewish homes.

The fact that Rick underwent few of these ceremonies but went to Sunday school and was confirmed is of no matter. Both of Rick's parents are Jews.

The rabbi said he felt it might be better for us to raise our children without religious education rather than to expose them to an ambivalent household. In fact, he added, he didn't even know if our child would be accepted into their Sunday school program. (They don't accept children who just want to learn about Judaism.) Or perhaps he'd be accepted but later be asked to leave.

Asked to leave! I was so angry when I heard that — a zinger he didn't mention until five minutes before he wound up our meeting — that I could barely speak. Talk about traumatic experiences! I can just see it. Pony's in first grade and the second year of Sunday school. It's still lots of fun; friends have been made. And, what, she asks too many questions? Says Mom puts up Christmas decorations but doesn't make a Seder dinner? And the decision is made by the school, by the rabbi, that Pony is not appropriate? Too disruptive? The rabbi wasn't clear under what circumstances they would ask the child to leave. I was so flabbergasted and horrified all my previous emotion evaporated. "You might not allow the child in school?" I repeated. To his face, I became the computer, simply gathering and processing information.

How would a child feel when he was told that he wouldn't be allowed to return to school? If he hated it anyway, it would be easy. Issues could be skirted. But what if he enjoyed it? How could we possibly explain? Because a child approached her religious education with an open mind, she'd be penalized.

Rick said nothing. As we left, he asked for a membership application and a phone number for someone in the interfaith marriage support group. Later, he said he thought the schooling comments were outrageous. If they ever kicked our child out of school, he said, he'd never set foot in that congregation again.

But that's a trauma, for both Pony and Rick, that I want avoided well in advance. I want to know, specifically, what criteria the rabbi was referring to for ejection from school. I do not want to subject Pony to the potential of that trauma. If that could happen, maybe we shouldn't enroll the child in the first place.

So the rabbi has presented us with a catch-22. Our original decisions on how to raise Pony are not acceptable to the Jewish faith. We have to do more or "the child will not be considered Jewish by any Jew." If it weren't for my resistance, Rick wouldn't be disturbed by the added ritual. He says he loves me most and doesn't want me to be unhappy. I come first. But if I remain adamant? Sunday school only, unless the child wants to do more? Then the child is an outcast, and I feel that Rick, deep down, would be distressed. It would be a compromise he'd live with, but it would have heavy consequences.

And me? If I give in, and promise to start with the *brit* ceremony on the eighth day and forced bar or bat mitzvah, will I constantly feel like a liar? At odds and alienated from my own family? Undermine the training anyway, by feeling forced to explain my views more forcefully to the children than if their Judaism were more low-key?

I had assumed that, religiously, our lives wouldn't change particularly with children. We'd take them to school but otherwise attend about the same number of services we attend now. The lack of home rituals would not change. The most Rick ever said, a few months ago, is that he might like to light candles at Friday dinner occasionally as Pony grew up. I was surprised, but said "sure."

In our discussions following this meeting with the rabbi, I learned more. Rick had assumed that children automatically change the religious life at home. While he agrees that he will be the basic initiator, he anticipates, *and has silently anticipated*, lots of change! The kids will come home from Sunday school with lots of assignments and activities. Celebrating certain holidays at home, for example. Of course we'd participate. There are lots of family activities involved in Sunday school, he says. Home life is bound to change.

Leaving me feeling betrayed. Angry at our lack of communication. Angry at Rick. Angry at the rabbi and the religion. Feeling that Rick will want to please me first but is simultaneously being pulled into this rigid structure; a structure in which he has not participated, in that manner, in the five years I've known him. And a structure he never talked about participating in.

July 22

It took me two days to regurgitate the above. There's more. More details, more tangents. Perhaps even more of import, but I'm played out. Those are the obvious emotional highlights.

Yesterday afternoon, I spent an hour and a half in a used bookstore poring over the religion shelves. Pulling off this book and that, mostly on Judaism, also looking for volumes on Unitarianism (which I couldn't find) and child-rearing chapters on raising children of mixed marriages.

I purchased three children's textbooks on Jewish history, from Abraham, the first Jew (I've learned something already), to the 1950s when they were published. The simplicity is just my speed, given my abysmal knowledge of all religious history. I bought them because I want to learn. Regardless of what happens with our children. Rick's memory is too faded; he can never answer any of my questions.

The lone chapter I found in another text was on mixed marriages in general, not child rearing in particular. If I had read it a week ago, I wouldn't have thought it pertained to us. Basically, it spoke of the hard work, patience, respect and compromise required in a relationship where two people don't share one faith. And how the presence of children magnifies one thousandfold all the effort required. It pointed out how people tend to downplay reality before marriage, instinctively wanting to avoid potentially disruptive issues. And how, often, people don't realize how strong their beliefs are until children come along.

Amen to that.

Yet what I had been looking for was ammunition to counter the "traumatic effects of the ambivalent household" argument made by the rabbi. Or, honestly, sources—even one—that supported him which might make me more comfortable with additions of household ritual. I found nothing.

Rick feels strongly about raising a child *one* thing or nothing. I hadn't realized that. I would be open to having the child attend religious education in two faiths. Rick thinks that would be too confusing. I'm not sure I agree that it would be confusing, but I do agree that it would increase the likelihood of the child growing into a freethinker and rejecting organized religion altogether.

It's interesting to me. As much as Rick has shared what problems and unhappiness existed in his first marriage, he neglected to mention something that, in today's context, seems important. He had told me that his first wife, an active Christian, had wanted any children they might have to be baptized and raised in her church. He didn't tell me until yesterday that she wanted the potential children raised in both her church and the Jewish faith. I can't help but wonder, didn't that come up before they married? It may have, but I believe Rick experiences the reality of a baby as I do, as something utterly new. My resistance to organized, orthodox religion is enhanced as much as Rick's commitment to Judaism is fanned by the impending presence of a life we are responsible for.

We have talking and reading and thinking yet to do. Suddenly we have to reexamine our values under the gun of an eight-week timetable (or less). We need to know what we want to do about a blessing on the eighth day of life *before* Pony is born!

July 26

I've been reading and reading. Jewish history, Jewish rituals, conversion to Judaism, comparisons of religions . . . ! I'm fascinated and enjoy the learning. Despite my ranting about organized religion (fear of narrow-mindedness and meaningless ritual), as I learn more specifics, I am left with two core concerns. How does Judaism, even Reform Judaism, square with feminism? And can a committed Jew question the existence of God?

While I'm comfortable understanding God as a vital force as opposed to some incarnate, personal God, sometimes I am left feeling even that unifying force idea isn't true. Although I embrace that abstraction most of the time, I firmly respect the doubts of agnostics and atheists. I believe it's reasonable to entertain questions. Rick says he thinks this is reasonable and acceptable in Judaism.

I was heartened to read in one source that some 40 percent of rabbis view God as a "vital force" and not a personal God, three percent doubt the existence of God, and one percent do not believe in God. These figures stand in stark contrast to Christian religions, where 90 percent of religious leaders believe in a personal God.

And the feminism? Comparatively, Judaism hasn't done too badly historically. Yet it so obviously carries the historical baggage of patriarchy. To explore this area further, I've sent for the current issue of *Lilith*, a feminist Jewish quarterly magazine.

There are certainly more questions. They increase as I read, but they also become less vague, more articulate. Rick is pleased that I'm so interested in learning more. He laughs that he's going to be pretty busy if he intends to stay apace.

There's more news about Pony that is fun and immediate. Last week, on the 19th, the midwife told us Pony is already in a head-down position. That was exciting. Besides indicating that a breech presentation is highly unlikely (they can rarely turn fully once into the pelvis with the head), it means, to us, that the end is closer than ever!

And Pony is named. If it's a boy: Joseph Ethan Glaser-Reich. If it's a girl: Anna Claire Glaser-Reich.

This morning I had the sweetest dream. It was long. I was giving birth. Rick and Ruth were there. Except for the lack of pain (I only felt discomfort), the dream was real. But pushing took the longest time. I didn't feel I was accomplishing much with my efforts, but finally she was born! When she was halfway out, she looked at me. Then they put her on my chest, and she raised her head again to look me in the eyes. She had a crop of dark hair and her eyes were large and light brown. Bronze, Ruth said. I was awed and tickled. This baby didn't have average baby eyes of blue. They were brown like her Daddy's. Lighter, of course, but brown. I nursed her then. She was quite proficient, but would still continue to pause and look up at me. It was wonderful.

July 29

Anna Claire was born. Annie. I couldn't believe how wonderful she was. How happy I was. Rick and I were home, in our bedroom. The cradle was bedside. She was beautiful. And so intelligent! She was only a few days old but she was able to say words and partial sentences. It was hard to understand, but she was talking. And there was another deeper level of communication between us. Verbal yet nonverbal. Our nursing was so intimate, so satisfying. I was amazed I could feel like this. I was awed and engrossed and fully in love.

There was some dream sequence involved. Routines of baby care and sleep. It was so very real. I nursed her again and, as I expected, she pooped in her diapers. Some came through on my pants. It was early in the morning, and I was still in bed with Rick. He brought me some tissues to wipe up. I told Annie and Rick I'd have to go change her diapers. I carried her down the hall to the nursery, and the scene subtly shifted. I wasn't aware of it at the time, but it was no longer our house but a larger place with other people around. I went into the nursery (which did look like ours) and saw that the changing table hadn't arrived but decided I could use the dresser top. Annie was still communicating, with and without words, delighted to be alive.

I grew nervous. I had never changed a diaper. They were cloth, and I didn't even know how to fold them! I found some pins on the dresser top and went back into the hallway. I asked an acquaintance for help; she was a nurse. We went back into the nursery and I lay Annie down on her back on the wooden dresser. But my hand was too low on her neck. A few inches above the surface, her head slipped backward and banged on the hard wood. I had a flash of panic, simultaneously telling myself this kind of thing happens and that she would be fine. Then some clear liquid bubbled and ran from her mouth and her eyes glazed over. I couldn't get her to talk.

I was horrified. Terrified. Screamed for a doctor. Hugging her to my body. First one doctor came, but he ignored the problem. He didn't even look at Annie. I ran outside to find another. An obviously competent doctor took her from me to examine her and to work on her. My fear was total. Rick was there then. I choked out the story of what I'd done. I was, and felt in the dream (nothing flat here), hysterical. Desolate. But clinging to hope. It was impossible Annie would die. We'd come so far. She was so wonderful. It couldn't happen.

Then I turned back. The doctor had covered her up. Completely. She was dead. I could only keen in despair and denial. Rick put his arms firmly around my shoulders, slowly walking me away from the corpse. Annie was now a corpse. He said I'd make it through this "transition." I'd work it through. He was doing his best to help. I only felt, through my very fiber, I could never get through it. Through the guilt of losing her by my incompetence. Through the gaping hole of having known her, adored her, and lost her.

On waking, all I could do was hold my tummy and tell myself it was only a dream. To try and feel reassured by her movements.

August 2

A busy weekend with Rick's three sisters and his Mom here for his birthday.

I'm tiring more easily; it's becoming more obvious. I'm sleeping later in the mornings again but feel I need the rest. Certain discomforts are increasing. I find myself short of breath, out of the blue. My heart races at 120 beats per minute, yet when I swim this isn't a problem. I believe the deep, rhythmic breathing prevents the windedness and palpitations. All the books say this is normal and so did Ruth at our appointment today.

Everybody—the visiting family, the women at the pool, people on the street—everybody thinks I look small for only seven weeks to go. It makes me nervous! My weight has plateaued at a 20-pound gain. Ruth pooh-poohed my fears. My uterus measured 34 centimeters today, right where it should be. "That baby's growing," she said.

We had to wait over an hour before she saw us today. Rick was getting restless although maintaining good spirits. Unfortunately, he fidgets with things (the stirrups, the light, the end of the table), and it makes me edgy. I told him labor should be more interesting; I hope it will be, or I might tie him in a chair to stop the fidgeting!

We learned the sad news when Ruth came in. She apologized for her lateness and explained that a woman had just lost her baby. "You just can't walk out on that," she said. No kidding. Was it the woman with the long dark hair I saw her lead back an hour before?

Or the blond who came in for an ultrasound? The suddenly absent heartbeat. No explanations available.

I can't believe it. More sad news. I just got a call from Brenda, the graphic artist who worked at *The Charleston Gazette* during my tenure as a reporter there. Tom K., a fellow reporter who moved on to the *Pittsburgh Post Gazette* after I left, is dead. He died this weekend in a car wreck near New York City. The car ahead of him on the freeway had a blowout. Tom was a young man. Our age — 30, maybe 32. Still single. A good reporter. A promising writer. How can he be dead?

Saturday was the 12-year anniversary of my father's death. I think this was the first time the day passed without my noticing.

August 4

My shortness of breath has improved today, perhaps because I've been taking the day slowly. This morning I finished the last hour of freelance writing that Mara subcontracted to me, and prepared it for delivery. Apart from that, I slept late, took a leisurely shower, caught up over the phone with Becky in Raleigh, fed the birds, read some more in a new book, *Basic Judaism*, and fielded a call from a woman in Charleston. She and her husband are thinking of moving here, and she wanted to pick my brain. As usual, I sounded like an ad from the chamber of commerce.

Rick's off to New Hampshire tonight for the weekend. A prep school friend he hasn't seen in more than 10 years asked him to be godfather to their third child. Rick wanted me to go but, when the arrangements needed to be made last month, I didn't think I would feel up to it. I'll miss him, and I probably could have gone without any great discomfort, but I'm just as glad not to add another layer of hectic activity.

August 5

Rick was so tickled watching Pony move two nights ago. On the way to the airport yesterday, he asked me if Pony moved like that during the day. I said yes, strong movement is common these days. "Did you watch?" he asked. "No," I replied, startled. "I think I'd watch all the time," he laughed, "it's amazing."

I think I've entered a denial phase of pregnancy. I'm spending hours reading on Judaism, women's spirituality, and fiction but no baby books. I've read some, but nothing recently. And I never even finished Dr. Spock. Blasphemous!

And Pony's movements? I vacillate. Sometimes I think it's really neat, and sometimes I feel overtaken, queasy, unnatural. Her movement can seem wonderful and integral, normal; and then again, simply weird.

August 8

I placed our order with the diaper service. They'll deliver the first 90 diapers, an average week's supply, on September 6th (two weeks before the expected due date).

Pony woke me this morning with hiccups. Gentle, regular. It felt more like tiny rhythmic kicks or pushes, but I understand that such a regular pattern indicates hiccups.

I wonder if Rick was shell-shocked by his weekend away with a family of three young children. He reported that the baby was cute, even though it cried a lot, and he told a story of how the four-year-old girl would ask him, "Weady, Wick?" (having a tough time with her r's) when they were playing in the lake. And how, when he jumped straight in the lake with his running shorts and sweat-soaked shoes, she asked him, "Was that a mistake?" Despite all this adorableness, he's also told me in a surprised and startled tone that the children's father is up at 6:00 a.m. everyday. And he added, with new fervor, "Children sure do change things."

I figure a little anxiety is good for him. I have few doubts that he'll take to fatherhood in a snap.

I love the way he kisses Pony through my tummy. Even though his beard scratches my stretched and sensitive skin, I wouldn't ask him not to or trade the experience for anything.

August 13

Restful sleep is harder to come by. I doze through the night, never completely comfortable, trying to prop up my protruding belly. And I am chased by complicated, endless dreams. I've begun napping from 6:00 p.m. until 8:00 p.m. when Rick comes home.

This morning, for the first time, I felt ready to birth this baby and get it on the outside.

Five weeks to go.

August 16

I find I'm avoiding these pages. I alternately think I'm fully adjusted to the coming of the baby and then that I'm using supreme efforts to suppress growing dread that something will go wrong at this late date. Those unexplained stillbirths.

The nursery is more or less complete. We could use some more equipment, and the layette needs filling out, but there aren't any gaping holes that can't be quickly filled.

I find myself walking to the end of the hall more frequently. I stand in the doorway or sit in the rocker Rick bought for me, just looking. Trying to imagine Pony in there. It's a comfortable, happy room. It feels ready.

We've put the cradle in our room, by the foot of the bed, as much to get us used to it as the dogs. Bruin still walks a wide circle around it and watches warily from a good distance if it actually rocks back and forth. Jessie doesn't seem to care.

My tummy measured out the same size today as two weeks ago,

but Ruth isn't concerned. She says babies in utero grow in fits and starts just like children. She again reassured me about the breathlessness and heart palpitations. I noticed my heart pounding at 138, at rest, today! She said that as long as it doesn't exceed 160 or last longer than an hour, it's normal. My acceleration is usually gone within 10 minutes.

We're in the home stretch. Now I'll see Ruth every week. And we begin the daily perineal massage at home, to lessen the likelihood of an episiotomy.

Emily told me a funny story last week in the locker room. She's due within days of me. We were discussing Durham County General, and she said a friend delivered her first child there and had moments of total panic. She was in hard labor when she heard another woman screaming bloody murder, shouting such things as, "Get your hands off me! . . . Stop it! . . . I can't breathe! Get your hands off me!!" The friend was horror-struck. What were they doing to this woman? What would they be doing to her? She later learned that the screaming woman was a *nurse* allegedly fending off a woman in labor!

A nice thing that's occurred during the last month has been a reconnection with Nancy. I wrote her a letter a few weeks after I got back from Portland and asked for her perceptions of our visit, sharing some of my own. She was relieved to know I had felt the disjointedness, as she had, too. She called me, and we discussed the possible contributing factors and moved on. She also proved to be a great ear for me in my initial throes of discontent about the rabbi and the religious upbringing of Pony. We didn't come up with any new answers, but talking to an objective uninvolved listener helped calm me down.

Rick and I saw a great VCR movie recently that reminded me of the woman on the street needing help in Portland. *House of Games* by David Mamet; the ultimate con. It showed me that the woman who approached me knew exactly what she was doing. Watching the movie about cons and double-cons while unraveling the psyche of the victim (later a con, of sorts, herself) was fascinating. Could I be conned again? Probably. If not, I think I would have to become forever suspicious of all human nature.

August 17

I bought Pony's first toy this week: a six inch tall, squishable teddy bear. I suppose Rick started collecting toys for our first child with our first pregnancy. He purchased a half-size, blue and white Duke basketball and, later, a miniature lacrosse stick. Both probably not worth much to the child until he or she is about two, but they were the start. I got all sentimental inside when I purchased the bear. I imagine that's how Rick felt when he purchased the sports toys.

August 18

I realize I've almost completely ignored one of the most disruptive, demanding issues of this pregnancy: religion. I've sidestepped active soul-searching in recent weeks by releasing my resistance to the first hurdle. We'll have whatever level of *brit* ceremony is necessary on day eight. I suppose I feel that I now have five years to keep thinking about it. Five years until school starts. We've joined the temple, which is not a major step. We've been members of one temple or another since we've been married.

As I review my thoughts of late July, I become agitated once again. My recent readings on feminist spirituality for the extension meetings of the ''Goddesses'' class renew my questions and resistance. Can Judaism truly embrace feminism? I still don't know, but my doubts are strong. This saddens me, but I'm far from giving up hope of finding my niche, one that's comfortable for me and the family. Part of me longs for a simple clear identity, a belonging to a group or clan. To simply say, ''I'm Jewish. My family is Jewish.'' I just don't know if I'll ever be able to do that.

August 26

I'm exhausted. Restful nights have been hard to come by. I sleep lightly, sensitive to Rick's every move. The baby may have dropped some, but not with any positive benefit to me. I have to get up twice a night to pee, and my shortness of breath and heart palpitations continue.

Tuesday I was thrilled to learn that I am already 90 percent effaced. The cervix is almost completely thinned out although dilation hasn't begun yet.

Ruth was delivering a baby so Dr. Fried did this exam. He cracked so many jokes I thought he was kidding when he first said I was 90 percent effaced! I sobered up and asked a few questions when I saw him write it in my chart. He assured us that my body is doing exactly what it's supposed to do and that I may be more likely to deliver during the two weeks before my due date than during the two weeks after. Yet he pointed out that he has seen women with good early effacement go to or past their due dates.

At each weekly appointment now, I'll be examined for a progress check.

Mom has been visiting this week, and we've had a good time although in periods of fatigue I don't feel like interacting with anyone. She attended Bradley class with us Monday and came to the doctor's office Tuesday and heard the heartbeat. (We've been joking since that she may be here for the delivery after all!) The medical news Tuesday prompted me to go out Wednesday and buy nearly everything else we need for the baby. I filled in the layette with kimonos, undershirts, and waterproof lap pads and bought a rocker-swing (a device recommended by innumerable parents). Mom bought us a playpen and high chair. She irked me, though, with her almost moral opposition to the swing. She didn't say a lot, but her dislike was obvious.

"Why do you have to put a baby in a *swing* all the time?" she sniffed.

"It's not for all the time," I say. "Parents can misuse any baby equipment: playpens, for example. But parents say they find this wonderfully soothing when babies cry."

"Just let them cry," Mom says.

And I felt like lashing out that we are not hiring nurses, like you did, to be substitute Mom and do the dirty work. We're going to be frontline parents, in good times and bad, and we may well need a little mechanical relief now and then. Sure babies will sometimes cry until everyone's blue in the face, but this baby's not going to want for skin-to-skin nurturing. I hardly think a baby swing is a cop-out.

My irrational irritation actually focused on those aspects of her mothering that I don't relate to: that we were bottle-fed, that she used full-time nurses for our care, and that she has often said she doesn't like babies. Perhaps I'm afraid that she won't (or can't) "be there" for me next month as a mentor or guide. Even if she knows the mechanics of helping, I don't want my role model to be one who disdains the process.

In spite of all this, there have been good times this week: mostly our discussions about religion, feminism, and spirituality. The extension of the "Goddess" class met this week and that was the topic I, as facilitator, had selected. Mom, who happened to be down here in April and attended the first class, had been doing some reading in the books we purchased then. *The Crone*, which discusses the historical shift from matriarchal to patriarchal culture, has especially piqued her interest particularly since author Barbara Walker focuses on society's bent for discounting and disregarding older women.

Mom also told me a little more about our family history of religious training (or lack thereof). She said my father had suggested we be sent to Hebrew Sunday school and she, "ever the rebel," challenged him on it. How could he explain his lack of belief to us while sending us to school? He let it go, but a few months later he told her he "wouldn't mind" if she wanted to send us to Catholic school. She hooted at that, having emphatically rejected that institution at 16.

Despite my father's atheism, born from his scientific training, Mom believes, he was envious of those who did have faith. She said he commented frequently at the time of President Kennedy's assassination on how Jackie Kennedy's faith helped her through. Although I was only 6 at the time, I remember those comments.

Both parents understood the value of community found in churches and synagogues.

They felt the strong anti-Semitism in Short Hills that was prevalent in the early 1960s and did their best to ignore it. Mom thinks Pop may have chosen to live in Short Hills to separate himself from his Jewish background. There were other nice areas to live in nearby, areas with larger Jewish communities.

Pop's desire, albeit not implemented, to give his children some religious community, some roots, draws me closer to him.

I still keep reading and reading.

One interesting parallel between the women's spirituality movement (with focuses on nature as well as the "Great Goddess") and Judaism is the fact that the Jewish calendar year is based on the cycles of the moon. There are monthly ceremonies engaged in by feminist Jews celebrating the new moon and the month ahead.

It is critical for me that Pony's religious training not instill, even obliquely, a view that women are inferior, secondary, or designed for domesticity. The universality of God, a God beyond the confines of any sex, and the strength and pride of womanhood with all the options inherent therein — this must be something that Pony (boy or girl) appreciates.

September 7

A gorgeous morning. Autumn is paying us a temporary visit. Cool, crisp, a ripe pungent feeling that you can't quite smell.

The birds empty the feeder with new gusto. As fall approaches we are visited by flocks of blue jays and blackbirds. A jay perches on a spindly branch calling to his fellows, a screech of a cry that moves briefly to a soft imitation of a melody before returning to its insistent pitch.

My sleep is calmer and deeper. Rick has decided to give the firm his all, plunging into civil work as they have requested. This is a relief to me. We still don't know what will happen in six months — whether they will be happy with Rick and whether he will be happy with them — but my worry is eased. I know how capable he is. If he works hard, he'll produce what they want. But we know there are no guarantees.

What is it that allows me to say that with a good measure of tranquillity? We learned that lesson last summer. Twelve weeks into a pregnancy isn't magic. Neither is 28. Neither is full term. You can lose your baby from your womb at any time, without explanation. You may birth a beautiful child who died moments before. You may take home a healthy squalling infant only to have it succumb to SIDS at a year, dying in its sleep, cause unknown. A healthy active toddler can drown in a few inches of water. Your five-year old can ingest Drano. Your seven-year old can be killed by an out-of-control automobile. Your rebellious teenager or brilliant college student could die in a car speeding toward a party or a weekend at the beach. You almost laugh at the list, shaking your head in amused disbelief. There is no magical safe point.

You can take precautions, but you cannot control.

And the internal precautions may be as important as the external. Refusing to engage, to bond, to feel, is a seductive path, an attempt at caution. It's hard to avoid that path. A sense of self-preservation can lead you that way despite the best of intentions.

The internal precaution to cultivate is a sense of immediacy and appreciation of life. Certainly one should forego entanglement in a web of discontent over the little things. To cultivate an ability to let go without losing sight of your goals and dreams. To be buffeted by the unexpected, understanding that it will happen when least anticipated, but to hold on tight, keeping an eye on a beacon of light however tiny and far away. To learn to lose what is dearest and to live again. This is what we work for, what we wait for.

I muse and wax philosophical in a sunny breeze-filled kitchen. Flowering geraniums and spider plants and pottery fill the bay window; gentle woods whisper outside. Despair seems so far away. I can only pray that the next time it hits I'll be able to hold on to some of what I've learned. I would like to believe that the cumulative effect of tragedies is not to progressively embitter, but to enhance one's sensitivity, flexibility, and wisdom.

EPILOGUE

Joey was born at 7:26 p.m. on September 15th. He was 21 inches long and weighed eight pounds even. I could only repeat an incredulous, "Oh my!"

Afterword

A common reaction to this journal has been, "I want more."

I want to know what happened during the birth and during those first days and months at home.

I want to know what you think other women in different economic classes face; how do they cope with identity issues, fatigue, lack of money? You speak from privilege. What about others?

I want to know how you really grieved. I especially want to know more about the second miscarriage. What happened? How did you grow from this and resolve it?

I would like to address all of these issues in addition to one or two of my own. Some I can answer, some I cannot.

This book, despite its casual style, is not a verbatim, raw journal. The first draft was written as such, but *Waiting* has undergone much editing and revising. However, I did want to maintain the integrity of the mind-set enveloping me at that point in my life, including my myopia, my selective vision, my lack of perspective. I have grown one thousandfold since the birth of my son in 1988. My view of nearly everything pertaining to life with child is now different. Not always radically so, but different.

Editing the work post-baby thus became a challenge. It's easy to forget how I felt and easier still, retrospectively, to want to make myself look like a better person than I was. (Goodness, did I really complain *that* much? Was I really that lazy? Was I actually overwhelmed with concern over the *nursery* decor!) The self-absorption I succumbed to during pregnancy was part of my experience. It may have been exacerbated by the two miscarriages. Although I never consciously blamed myself for them, I may have been watching my every move, ad nauseum, because of them.

Many issues, certainly those of import, transcend socioeconomic status. Neither rich nor poor have cornered the market on anxiety or grieving. When one is fortunate enough to be free of worry over money for rent and food, one has time to become more reflective and, consequently, sometimes more self-absorbed. Solutions to many "problems" easily present themselves. Time for oneself? Time as a couple? Hire babysitters. The same issues are likely to arise for working-class and poverty-level mothers, too, but the issues might be ignored because it is more important to figure out how to stretch the family income to cover diapers and formula. If time and energy allow a poor mother to raise the question, "What about me?" she must seek other solutions. Friends, family, neighbors, babysitter co-ops: all are ways to buy time without financial cost.

Such found time, claimed time, for any mother may be most fruitfully spent taking a nap or soaking in a bath. Can a woman struggling economically feel enough validity to do such things for herself or does such behavior feel trivial and self-centered? Will she take care of herself in the face of so many fundamental pressures?

As a woman raised with economic privileges, working as a writer and not a research sociologist, I cannot answer those questions. But I do feel that all women should remember to find a way to take care of themselves and not to submerge themselves completely in the caretaker role.

That this journal is entrenched in an overly middle-class point of view is but one concern. A more common question has centered on the second miscarriage and my grieving and mourning process. Where the first miscarriage was so clearly etched in my mind, its aftermath and the entire second miscarriage have remained only a haze. All the details I can muster have been recorded in the journal.

I, too, remain surprised at the void there. I think the process of writing down all that I could remember, coupled with preoccupation about the ever more visible new life, ultimately released me from the pain of those losses. I can speculate that, despite my best efforts, I never resolved my grief. That I buried it to move on with my life. While not the course of choice, it may have occurred despite my best efforts to confront my losses directly. How often this might mirror others' grieving, again, I don't know. I write this book not to give a model of behavior or insight, but to share the sly and sometimes insidious workings of one mind, body, and soul during the transition to motherhood. I feel I *have* settled with the past and put the ghosts of memory and pain to bed, not buried them in the closet.

My spiritual journey, too, has flourished since the doors were flung open during pregnancy. A large part of the "Goddess" class still meets on a regular basis to explore feminist spirituality. And I now pursue this aspect of spirituality as a Jew. Months of research and soul-searching allowed me to claim my identity as a Jew — a feminist Jew — but a Jew. I converted when Joey was one year old. I converted for myself, not for Joey, not for the family.

This spiritual development, and a concurrent growth of friendship, in some ways illustrates as profoundly as a baby's development that life is change. John Friedman, the rabbi who acted as a lightning rod for my anger and frustration, is the rabbi I chose to study with for conversion. John was strong enough and foresighted enough to risk my wrath by forcing us to look at the hard questions; questions that might well have been skirted to our own detriment. John's supportiveness to interfaith families is exemplary. He also has subsequently explained that the school attendance issue was more reflective of ongoing discussions by the Board of Trustees (of which I am now a member) than his own point of view.

My transition to motherhood was a bumpy one, replete with loss and grief, but was the first step on the journey of expanding my self-image from woman to mother. Of course the final step in the transition is actually *being* a mother! This seems a never ending process that begins when you first lay eyes on your baby and, I surmise, does not end even if your child precedes you in death. Being a parent is something so different that I feel one can only truly know it by experiencing it. To try to capture the experience with words would be a worthy task, but that of a different book.

I do wish with all my heart to tell my son how much I love him. That despite the exhaustion, frustration, and boredom that can be part of the job, I adore him and the challenge he presents. Catch me at a bad moment and I'm ready to chuck it all. But give me a moment of quiet, and I can't imagine not sharing my life with him in the way I do.

Index